A
Guide
to
Western
Civilization

Joe Bob Briggs (signature)

By the same author:

JOE BOB GOES TO THE DRIVE-IN

A
Guide
to
Western
Civilization,
or
My Story

by JOE BOB BRIGGS

Delacorte Press

Published by
Delacorte Press
The Bantam Doubleday Dell Publishing Group, Inc.
666 Fifth Avenue
New York, New York 10103

Chapters 1, 2, 7, and 15 originally appeared in **National Lampoon** magazine in slightly altered form.

Library of Congress Cataloging in Publication Data

Briggs, Joe Bob.
   A guide to Western civilization, or My story / Joe Bob Briggs.
      p.   cm.
   ISBN 0-385-29671-1
   I. Title. II. Title: My story.
   PS3552.R458G85   1988
   813'.54—dc19   87-36424
                                                      CIP

Manufactured in the United States of America

July 1988

10 9 8 7 6 5 4 3 2 1

BG

Contents

A
Guide
to
Western
Civilization

1

Life with the Indians

You probly never been out to Krankaway County, Texas. I don't blame you. It was named after the Krankaway Indians, which you might of heard about as the ones that ate dung beetles for breakfast and rammed crooked sticks through each other's arms to see who was more macho, but they had this problem of being so incredibly stupid they never did learn to ride horses and so after a while the Comanches came down from Boise or wherever it was up there and they wiped out all the Krankaways in six hours fighting. You may be wondering why it took six hours, and the reason is the Krankaways *did* learn to ride goats, which was proved by some goat bones which our county historian, Thedadean Nguyen, found out by the scenic overlook. A lot of people that used to believe this don't believe it anymore, ever since Thedadean married one of the boat people that moved in from Vietnam to work on the Stiles Farm, but I witnessed some of those bones my ownself and I can verify that those goats were killed with warlike weapons. Either that or some of the boys from the high school got drunk and shot up some goats with their twenty-twos. Also, some of them bones don't look so much like goats as they look like big old huntin dogs. I told this to Thedadean to try to set the record straight, but she said in her opinion, based on all the evidence she could find, the Krankaway Indians never did learn to ride big ole huntin dogs. Anyhow, the Comanches turned all the Krankaways into human oatmeal in what we call the Six Hours of Shame and nobody knows exactly why the Comanches did it. Based on some of the pictures I've seen, though, they probly killed em for being ugly. I don't mean to get into racism here, but those people were uglier than a set of Woolco lawn furniture.

As you can see, I'm a historical sort of person, being born in the West and all. Krankaway County is one of the last places in Texas that *is* West, now that I mention it, cause all the rest of the West has moved off into New Mexico. And let's face it, even those people are startin to get chewed on from the East. Last time I went to Albuquerque I saw one of those indoor shopping malls that looks like a giant Kleenex box with a bunch of fern bars stuffed inside it. And far as Santa Fe goes, forget it. Santa Fe is the best example in the U.S.A. of why we oughta forget the whole thing and give the sucker back to the Indians. The Comanches might of smelled bad, but at least they didn't go to graduate school in sociology so they could learn how to make turquoise ankle bracelets for homosexuals and talk to the farm animals in Buddhist.

Where I lived in Krankaway County is thirty-two miles from the New Mexico border, which I know exactly cause that's how far I had to drive to get three-two beer. In that part of Texas the Babtist church pretty much passes all the laws, but over in New Mexico they have enough Meskin votes so you can get this watered-down stuff that tastes like cranberry juice that's been filtered through a polyester pants suit. It was bottled by a guy in Lovington, New Mexico, under the label of Vision Beer, because the guy thought the Indians wouldn't drink nothing unless they thought they'd see some snakes or some barracudas or something. We used to bring these Vaseline cocktails back across the border by the case, then we'd go out behind the shed and puke it up and tell each other what a hell of a kick it had. We didn't know it at the time, but it didn't have no kick at all. About all Vision Beer had in it was natural-grain laxatives. We'd generally have to get off from school a couple days ever time we tried it.

It's incidents like that that made me say to myself the other day, "You know, you have a story to tell, Joe Bob," and then I realized how ridiculous it is to talk to yourself in quotation marks and I stopped doing that. It was that very day I decided to write this book. Or it may of been the day after that or the day before. But I want you to understand that this is gonna be the first completely true honest biography of a human bein you ever read, and the way I'm gonna do that is by never stayin on the subject. The *reason* I'm gonna do that is that Life never stays on the subject.

So don't expect any plot in this mother. If there's one thing I can't stand it's a plot. If you ever see a plot creeping into this baby, just rip out the page and send it in to me and I'll refund the page with the offending plot removed. The only thing I hate worse than plot is redeeming social value. I'm only gonna put one sentence of socially redeeming value in this whole book, and that's only in case the U.S. Supreme Court asks my lawyer to come up with it so we don't get banned in Meridian, Mississippi, which used to be a great town before the Babtists took hold of it.

Okay, here's my sentence:

"Look both ways before crossing."

Now the censors can't touch me, cause if they do, *innocent children might die.*

I'll probly cover the whole history of the world before we get through, but I want you to know in case you think I'm showing favoritism that I'm mainly intersted in the Western part of it. I'll tell you how come. Before I was born my daddy, Robert Bob Briggs, used to take my mama to this roadhouse called "Sharon's Crossing" on Farm-to-Market 2401, smack dab on a county line out south of Odessa somewhere, one of those places where you have to drive fifty, sixty miles for a cup of coffee. Mama or Daddy neither one was ever good at math, and so they happened to be at this place on the night when I started coming into the world, and Sharon Tankersley, the owner of the place, knew there was no way to risk a pickup ride all the way to Odessa, specially since there wasn't any water between there and the city, and so to make a long story short I was born right there in Sharon's Crossing while everbody was getting sloshed. So far *no problema.* But next morning, when they called the Justice of the Peace to come over and fix up the birth certificate, he said, "What part of the structure was the child born in?"

And everbody said, "What?"

And he said the roadhouse was the county line and he needed to know what the heck county I was born in. And so my daddy said what's the difference, and the J.P. starts in about how we were standing in the town of Civilization, Texas, but due to the local liquor laws, half of Civilization was in a dry county (the Eastern half) and the other part was wet as a greased javelina hog. In Eastern Civilization the awl binness had took over everthing, and all the three-piece suits from Texaco and Mobil had come in and built suburbs and straightened out the roads and put up some big old ugly Babtist churches where the trailer parks used to be and lowered the speed limit to 75 and cleaned up all the Sin. But over in Western Civilization they hadn't found any awl yet and so a man could still do any damn thing he pleased and they still knew how to cook *huevos rancheros* in the mornin and even the cows wore "Miller Time" T-shirts.

7329

732

0KVOTW003N9B

Title	A GUIDE TO WESTERN CIVILIZATION
Condition	Acceptable
Location	Walden Aisle A Bay 04 Item 7329
Description	May have some shelf-wear due to normal use.
Source	Prescanned
SKU	0KVOTW003N9B
ASIN	0385296711
Code	9780385296711
Employee	Irryadere
Date Added	10/8/2021 7:27:54 AM

I gotta give credit to my daddy, he didn't hesitate one minute, he just said, "Western side," and that was it. I wasn't only a Westerner by birth, I was a Westerner by *choice.*

I never have been back to Civilization, but they tell me the western part's all tore down now and the eastern part's about to go condo and so there's no reason to go look at it anyhow. But even though I never did see it with my own personal eyes, I think I got a lot to say about Western Civilization, specially the part that's not there anymore. And I got a lot to say about Eastern Civilization, which is just about everwhere you look. And I got another reason for writing this book, too. I think I can send this in to a book publisher in New York City and get a big pile of money.

I'll probly leave out a lot of stuff as I go along, specially in the years in the history of the world before I got famous, but don't worry about it cause you won't know the difference anyway.

Anyhow, I'm gonna assume you never been to Krankaway County, Texas, and go ahead and tell you about it. Our chief industry is dirt. We have more dirt per capita than any county in Texas, and one year we got wrote up in *Texas Highways* magazine as "Dirt Capital of North America." You name the dirt and we got it. We got red dirt, black dirt, clay dirt, dirtballs, rocky dirt, granulated dirt, a rare strain of Siberian tundra dirt, designer dirt, and special commercial dirts for your dirt-consuming industries. You can stand out on the northern edge of town looking up toward Oklahoma and Colorado and all you can see for miles is dirt. *Dirty Man's Weekly,* the international journal of the dirt business, is published downtown on the second floor of One Sod Place. Of course, I didn't know all this at the time I was living there.

When you grow up in Krankaway County, you take dirt for granted.

My daddy worked in the dirt mines. He first went down into The Pit in 1943, when they needed so much extra dirt for the war effort, and they paid him fifty cents a day and as much dirt as he could haul home in his pickup. He never complained, but I always thought Daddy hated the dirt mines, specially when he'd come home at 10 or 11 o'clock at night and track mud all over the linoleum. Mama would get a pained expression on her face, like it was about to break her, but she never would fuss. She understood. She'd married a dirt miner. And even if she had to go through her whole life without anybody in the family being clean, she could handle it.

A lot of people looked down on us because we were dirty all the time. Nothing seemed to help, not even Life-buoy. Mama did her best to make us look nice. All our clothes were dark brown—dark brown shirts, dark brown pants, dark brown shoes, dark brown dresses for my little sister. Of course, most of the time we couldn't afford clothes, so we used to go to school nekkid except in the wintertime. I think it hurt Mama that nobody ever could tell whether we had clothes on or not.

Me and my little sister had to walk eighty-four miles to school ever day. At night we'd read the *Pilgrim's Progress* by a gas lamp until we went to sleep, and then we'd be up at five in the morning fixing flapjacks for breakfast. I don't know why we did this. We shoulda ridden the school bus like everbody else and used the electric lights in our room, but Daddy said that's the way he did it and his daddy before him and his daddy before him, and so we agreed that we would grow up better people if we did it the stupid way. I guess we got up to about page 28 of the *Pilgrim's Progress,* since nobody can read more than two sentences at a time without falling dead asleep, but that book taught me a whole heck of a lot about capital letters. We always had to throw out the flapjacks, though, cause nobody in the family ever got out of bed before nine o'clock.

At the time I'm talking about, during the fifties, the Texas Legislature voted the state officially racist, which caused us a lot of problems in Krankaway County. We had everthing out there—Meskins, Indians, ugly white people, and coloreds. (I say "coloreds" cause that's what we called em then. It wasn't till the seventies that I started callin em Negroes.) We even had some Japaheenos that got trucked up from Fort Bliss when the war broke out, and six or seven people of the Jewish persuasion that came over from Lubbock and opened up a dirt brokerage company, and one old fart named Mr. Tolliver Gristle. Nobody ever did figure out what Mr. Gristle was, cause he stayed holed up in the house all day working on his clock collection and writing letters to the editor of the *Krankaway Krescent* about how the Germans were re-arming and there would probly be a blitzkrieg through Krankaway County within six months and it would be the first sign of the Anti-Christ and the Fiery Destruction of Texas and the only people who would last it out and be Raptured Up into the Heavens would be the ones who "kept the Hour of the Coming" as it was written in The Book. Mr. Gristle had evidently been reading in the *Pilgrim's Progress* himself, cause he could use capital letters like a son of a bitch.

Most people thought Mr. Gristle was missing a few face cards, but I always liked the old fart, mainly cause he didn't give a hoot. Sometimes he'd go down to the meetings of the Daughters of the Texas Confederacy, walk in, drop his pants, and walk out again. This created quite a show, mainly cause the only hair Mr. Gristle had left on his whole body was a little Burl Ives beard hanging off his chin by a thread. The man was a 74-year-old Hare Krishna

Kojak, and you don't want a person like that dropping his
pants when you're around. Thedadean Nguyen tried to
get him arrested for it three or four times, cause she said it
was causing a decline in attendance, but Sheriff Nogales
said he couldn't do a damn thing since it was a public
meeting and Mr. Gristle never did say anything or expose
"the actual fleshy part of his male thing" and so his behavior was covered under the First Amendment. I always
believed in the First Amendment, specially the protec-
tions it provides to professional liars.

Like I say, the Legislature voted Texas racist and we
didn't know what the heck to do. I woulda been happy to
get up a posse of wranglers and go hassle some minority
groups, but when you got a county full of dirt miners, you
can't hardly tell the difference. For example, one day we
went out to The Pit while they were hoisting the miners
up the shaft for lunchbreak, and one by one I'd say to em,
"What racial persuasion are you?"

And most of em would say, "Huh?"

But all the ones that didn't say "Huh?" would say, "I'm a
white man."

And this went on damn near an hour till this one ole boy
said, "I'm a white man," and somebody yelled back over
at him, "You're bout as white as a Tennessee roothog!"

And the miner in question got all steamed and yelled
back, "Hell you say!"

And I got all steamed myself and yelled, "What color's a
goldurn Tennessee roothog?"

And the challenger walked up and wiped a big old
handful of driller's mud off his chin and flung it down on
the ground and said, "A Tennessee roothog is the color of
one of those stalagmites in Carlsbad Caverns that has the
little titties on the top of it."

Now the alleged non-white person was really getting
p.o.ed, and so he dropped his dirt-mine helmet and wiped

enough black dust off his eyelids so he could stare at Tennessee Roothog, and he fixed him with a glare and then, real quiet-like, but steady as a rock, he said, "Those ain't stalagmites, they're *stalactites.*"

I think that's about when the horse manure started to fly. For the next half hour we had Dueling Dirtheads, with these two reform-school dropouts trying to settle who was whiter by beating the bejabbers out of each other. They kicked up so much ground with their boots that they made a little mushroom cloud over The Pit, and a lot of valuable dirt drifted over into Yoakum County, and when the foreman found about it he docked their pay and made em bust clods for two weeks. But by that time a lot of the dirt miners had money riding on the results, so one Saturday afternoon we all went down to the volunteer fire station so both these guys could be hosed down and we could see what color their skin was. When we got finished, Tennessee Roothog turned out to be a fellow named Stub Jenks who was originally from Lonoke, Arkansas, and judging by his face, he was definitely one hundred per cent pure dee white trash, probly descended from a long line of cousins. The other guy's name was Bobo Rodriguez, and sure enough, he was roughly the color of Taster's Choice Decaffeinated, so we didn't know what the heck he was.

"Bobo," I said to him, "things aren't looking too good for you in the *white* department."

Bobo stared at his arms for a few seconds, and then he said, "Oh yeah, I forgot. I'm not white. I'm a Shawnee."

We were none too pleased to find this out, specially since none of us had ever seen a Shawnee before and so we didn't know what one was *supposed* to look like. Sheriff Nogales said it was a little scary to think about when you realized there might be more Shawnees working in the dirt mines and who knows what we might find out if we hosed everbody down and checked for race.

Mr. Gristle had wandered over from his Clock House, and he said he thought it might be a conspiracy. After all, what were the odds of hosing down just two guys out of all the people that lived in Krankaway County and one of em turns out to be a Pawnee?

"Shawnee," said Bobo.

"Shawnee, Pawnee," said Mr. Gristle, "I say he's the Anti-Christ."

Several of the men wanted to send for Thedadean Bowser (this is when she was still married to T.L. Bowser, head of the rural electrical co-op for the greater tri-county area) to ask if there was ever a Shawnee or Pawnee in the county, but we were afraid Thedadean might be inclined to bring along her three-volume county history and read passages from it. (If you'd like to check it out of the library yourself, the titles are *Six Hours of Shame, Anglo-Saxon Pioneer Families of Krankaway County,* and *The City That Dirt Built.*)

What we finally decided was one Pawnee more or less didn't mean diddly to the Texas Legislature, and even if it did, we had no idea what to charge him with. We talked a little bit about building some separate restrooms and drinking fountains with little signs on em that said "Pawnees and Shawnees Only."

"Might as well just write Bobo Rodriguez on there if we're gonna do that," the Sheriff said.

But nobody thought it was a very good idea to give Bobo his own personal drinking fountain and restroom, even if he was a Shawnee, and judging by the look on his face, I believed him anyway.

"Hell, he just forgot what race he was," I said.

"Yeah, that's right," somebody else said, "he just forgot."

"Well," the Sheriff told Bobo, "don't let it happen again. Next time you forget your race *or* skin color, I'm turning in a full written report to the Texas Department of Public Safety and you'll be one sorry-looking Pawnee."

"Shawnee," said Bobo.

"He's the Anti-Christ," said Mr. Gristle.

"And Joe Bob," the Sheriff said.

"Yessir."

"I don't want to see any more of these men hosed down in public, is that understood?"

"Yessir."

"Especially not with Christmas dirt shipments comin up."

"Yessir."

The Sheriff knew my mama worked down at Pearl's Dirtworks during the holidays, making up gift packages that were sent all over the world.

It was my first brush with the law, but I think it taught us all a valuable lesson about Western Civilization, which was

The color of our skin might be different, but the color underneath our skin is disgusting.

It also taught me how, no matter what, they'll always blame it on you.

2

Frontage Road, Texas, or My Sex Life

The actual town I grew up in was named Frontage Road, Texas, and there wasn't hardly nothing there except us and a few Pawnee shacks. (After the Bobo Rodriguez incident, we took to using "Pawnee" for anybody who wasn't an obvious white man.) It was a company town, I guess, since everbody worked for one of the three big dirt exporters: Consolidated Dirt, Dirt General, and Earth Products International. My daddy always worked for Consolidated, even though he got offers all the time from the other two, because he liked the quality-control they had. I remember in 1951 the Dirtworkers of America went out on strike and President Truman was threatening to send in the National Guard to Krankaway County and dirt was scarce all over, and a dirt-hauler buddy of ours named Scrim Wilks came by hauling about a half a pickup of No. 7 topsoil and offered to share some of it with us, but Daddy recognized it right away as EPI dirt and he told Scrim, "I won't have that crap in my yard." That's the way my daddy was, and I think it had a permanent effect on me. To this day, I won't use nothing but Consolidated dirt, even if it means paying more.

Speaking of Scrim Wilks and dirt, Scrim had a daughter named Dede. Dede Wilks was about six years older than me and lived over in Bison, the county seat, and I'd see her at church and at school and whenever I did see her she'd raise her dress up over her head and act like it happened by accident, like in the Marilyn Monroe movie where Marilyn's skirt gets caught in the updraft and turns into a midget parachute. Dede was the first girl I really knew in the Biblical sense. By the time I was seven years old I'd seen more of this girl from the waist down than vice versa, and frankly, there wasn't much down there to look at.

"Dede Wilks," I said to her one time, "how can I talk to you when you have your dress up over your hairdo all the time?"

She answered me back but I couldn't understand cause her voice was muffled by her dress.

I don't wanta dwell on Dede Wilks cause there's not much to dwell on, but you're gonna see in a minute why this was important. Dede was a tall girl with light red hair (I think) and a tiny little waist and freckles on her arms and legs and pigtails and she liked to wear frilly things and ankle socks and penny loafers and she had hooters the size of Minnesota. Now I know it's not polite to talk about somebody's hooters in public, specially when the hooters in question aren't available for inspection, but I figure anybody that paid $9.95 for this book deserves all the abuse that comes your way. (If you didn't pay $9.95, or if you have a local library that was sick enough to buy this book, then you oughta be ashamed of yourself. If you paid $10.95, you got screwed.) Anyway, Dede Wilks had nuclear boobs.

(I forgot to mention before, but this is the sex chapter, so don't leave it lying around where your little perverted children can read it.)

Now I don't want any snickering when I say this, do you hear me? Because I'm trying to make a serious point here. The fact was that Dede Wilks had collapsible breasts. We're talking thirty-eights one day and Dixie cups the next. In fact, they were the most tempermental Ta-Ta's I

ever saw this side of Printer's Alley in Nashville, where
they had this stripper named Heaven Lee who had hers
trained to serve cocktails. I realize it's a sad thing when
human beings have to go through their whole life with
physical handicaps, but what the hey, you never know
what modern medicine is gonna come up with, and I even
suggested to Dede Wilks's mother one time that they
might send her to the Scottish Rite Hospital for Crippled
Children in Dallas to see what they could do to stabilize
that garbonza dystrophy before we had a poster child on
our hands. In the meantime Dede had to put up with a lot
of kid's talk—you know, harmless things really, but the
kind of remarks that hurt you inside when you're young.
Like Danny Bivens, he used to say *"Hey, Dede, where'd
you get them trick titties?"* And we all knew that Danny
didn't *mean* anything by it, but sometimes it would make
Dede cry at school and old Miz Perryman would have to
hold the boys in at reecess and give us a lecture.

"We have a *few* people in this class," she'd start off,
"who don't have any respect for the feelings of others. For
your information, Dede has a glandular problem . . ."

And as soon as she said the word "glandular," I would
usually send a spray of spit five rows across the room and
start to coughing and that would get everbody else going
and by the time Miz Perryman got to the end of the
sentence her face would look like somebody took the skin
off and turned it inside out, and the end result would be
that me or Danny Bivens or both of us would get sent to
the principal's office so our behinds could be kicked "from
here to North Dakota and back, young man."

Then for the next week we'd all play Gland Patrol. The
way you play Gland Patrol is somebody goes out in the
hall before school starts and they're the Lookout. The
Lookout has the responsibility of estimating hooter size
on sight and before Dede Wilks gets to her classroom. As

soon as the Lookout gets a fairly accurate reading, he writes the numbers on the end of the blackboard while Miz Perryman's not looking. A typical readout on Monday morning might be something like 34C+1, which we would all recognize immediately as the international symbol for "Right breast 34 inches, C cup; Left breast 35 inches, C cup," or if it was a different cup size on the left one the readout would have one more letter on it. What's important to remember is that this is the official Vegas betting line and will remain constant throughout the school day.

Next thing, I open the bank for bets of up to 35 cents per kid, cause 35 cents is usually all they had for lunch and two milks, and I'd pocket the 5 per cent juice on losers. The way it worked was we'd have four daily over/unders —one for each reecess, one for lunch, and one at the end of the day. At the appointed time—say about 10:45 for morning reecess—the Lookout would make the day's second calculation and write the correct numbers directly below the original numbers on the blackboard. So it would look like this here:

34C+1

35D−1 Even

. . . which is pretty self-explanatory. Between 8:30 and 10:45 Dede gained one inch and one cup on the right, held steady on the left but added a left cup. The house pays "over" bets on the right, takes a 5 per cent juice on "unders," pays cups-only bets on the left, and you'd have a fairly high Daily Double combination here due to the odd behavior of the left titty. But by now you're probly wondering, what happens to the under-over wagering on the left side only? Answer: House rakes it. Now we also had your specialty betting, which could be several combos throughout the day, including the Exacta (four over/unders in a row), the Maxwell House (eight bets, cups only), and the Betsy Ross (overs, unders, cups and sizes, for a total of 13 separate bets). And we had some ladies' bets, for the two or three girls who could toss in a few pennies. Their favorite bet was the Dumbo the Flying Elephant, which was a wager that Dede would balloon up to full size at least once during the day. If somebody ever hit a Betsy Ross, I might have to pay out thirty, forty bucks at a time, so you can see this got into the steep green. Danny Bivens, who was the usual Lookout and got 1 per cent off the top for handicapping, told me one time that we should take side-bet action on nipple erections, too, but I told Danny no way, José. That would be cruel.

"What do you think Dede Wilks is?" I yelled at him. "A piece of meat?"

I liked Danny, but sometimes he could be insensitive to the feelings of others. Besides, Dede Wilks didn't get nipple erections more than three, four times a week, and I couldn't figure out a way to make odds on it.

I know what you're thinking, though. You're thinking we were taking money on rigged garbonzas. You're thinking Dede Wilks was a walking foam-rubber factory and all we were doing was altering the dairy equipment at various times during the day. Of course I had to deal with this accusation quite a bit, specially from Slopehead Frammolino, this geek Pawnee from over in Bison who never did put down more than a nickel at a time. I had to bar Slopehead twice cause he kept coming to school early so he could hang around out on the highway, get a good look at Dede Wilks *before* she got there, and then go make side bets with the first-graders on what the Vegas line would be for the day. Then, if Slopehead lost any jack, he'd start yapping about faked-up boobies.

First of all, it just don't make scientific sense. It may be possible to shrink foam rubber a couple bra sizes if you mashed it down with bricks or stapled it up, but I went and asked Mr. Godbey the science teacher whether it would be possible to take a foam-rubber-padded brassiere and enlarge it substantially in any given eight-hour period without doing structural damage to the bra proper, and Mr. Godbey said basically to get my butt out of his office before he dissected me like a bullfrog.

Second thing is, even if we had the ability to manipulate Dede Wilks's chest measurements at will, there wasn't any point in it cause we were taking six points anyhow and I was already pocketing enough change for my college education.

Third thing, Dede Wilks was a member of the Krankaway County Spirit of Holiness Pentecostal Church, and I don't know how much you know about Pentecostals, but those people don't believe in any kind of ornamentation or artificial device being used at any place on their bodies.

Fourth thing is, I checked em.

I had to. This was becoming the kind of nasty rumor that can just destroy a small businessman, and it had to be put to a stop. The daily handle was starting to fall off and Danny Bivens wasn't speaking to me.

"You had your chance to check em already," Danny said, "and you didn't check em."

Danny was right. I was ashamed of myself. I let those melons slip right through my fingers.

You see, I did it out of a misplaced sense of morality. I was a very moral individual even as a child. I remained a virgin till I was nine years old, but I don't ever get any credit for it. I might as well been tomcatting around town all those years for all the good it did my reputation. It was Dede Wilks that screwed things up royally, when she got tired of just lifting up her dress over her head and so one day she offered me five bucks if she could "do anything she wanted to down there." I told her for five bucks she could airmail my private parts to Bora Bora. So she hauled me out to the Valhalla Drive-In on the federal highway between Muleshoe and Sudan, deflowered me on the backseat floorboard of some piece-of-crap Studebaker, and then told everbody and his dog that I raped her. Hell, I didn't hardly have anything to rape her *with*. That's when I learned my first lesson about sexual relations, which was, nookie never comes along when you want it to.

The only reason I'm throwing in this story now is cause as soon as I got back, Danny Bivens was waiting on me over at the dirt refinery, all nervous cause Dede was a big girl and he didn't know whether I'd survive it or not. After I told him the story—what I could remember of it, since it all happened so fast I didn't know nothing except it was the night they were showing Marlon Brando in *The Wild One*—Danny kind of smiled and said, "Well?"

And I got a grin on my face like I just bought a burlap blanket from a Pawnee, and I said, "What?"

And Danny started laughing, he was about to explode, and he said it again: "Well?"

And I didn't realize what the hell was going on, and so I said, "Huh?"

And this was getting awful boring, so Danny Bivens said to me, *"What did the groceries feel like?"*

And then I realized what he was talking about, and I had to say, "Oh, I forgot."

Danny was so disgusted he wanted to scissor off my gazebos, and the only way I talked him out of it was by saying I'd go back into the snake pit the following week and find out for sure. The only thing was, I refused to go back to the Valhalla Drive-In, cause Dede could get pretty rough and when you're nine years old you don't know for sure how much punishment you can take down there before it completely falls off.

So I come up with this alternate plan No. 2, which I called the Sneak Dogpile.

We had this thing at school where during the day at any time for whatever reason you wanted to do it, you could just yell out "Dogpile on Frankie," and everbody that heard you yell it would go jump on Frankie Sullivan and continue to sit on him until he quit struggling. This was one of my favorite childhood sports. Sometimes if you yelled it at just the right time, you could get twenty or twenty-five guys on top of Frankie and he'd plumb disappear in the pile. Sometimes we'd do "Dogpile on Slopehead Frammolino" or "Dogpile on Gary Krupps," but mostly we dogpiled on Frankie Sullivan cause he was more fun. Frankie never did figure out that if you just kept your mouth shut during the actual dogpiling you'd only have to go through it one time, but he couldn't stand it so ever time we'd get off he'd start screaming about his civil rights or the Golden Rule or something and then he'd go tell his mother and she'd have to call up the school and say something like, "My son claims that about twenty of the little fourth-graders sat on him yesterday and bent the lock on his Bambi lunchbox." But the other thing Frankie never did figure out was when that many guys are involved, there's *no way* to identify the one individual who originally yelled "Dogpile on Frankie." Normally about all that would happen is Miz Perryman would give us a speech about "rough-housing on the playground" and we'd have to sit there and ask questions like "Did something unfortunate happen to Frankie, Miz Perryman?"

Ever once in a while Frankie would get brave enough to say, "Danny Bivens yelled out 'Dogpile on Frankie' and then everybody jumped on me."

When this happened I would have to say something

like, "Surely you don't believe that twenty individual human beings with minds of their own would choose to jump on Frankie at exactly the same moment for no apparent reason. What's the motive?"

I could usually get her on motive. Frankie didn't understand that either. Kids don't ever have motives.

Okay, so here's what the Sneak Dogpile plan was. We had it set up for afternoon recess, which was the time when Dede Wilks usually hung out over by the Dwight D. Eisenhower Playground. (We had two playgrounds. One was the Ike Playground, where all the equipment was set up for physical fitness like a U.S. Marine obstacle course so they could train the eight-year-olds of America to fight the Russians, and it cost Krankaway County several million bucks. The other playground was called "The Playground." It had monkey bars, swingsets, seesaws and merry-go-rounds. We basically used the Ike Playground for chunking rocks.) Ordinarily I would be avoiding the Ike Playground in the afternoon, cause Dede used to take ever opportunity to throw her dress up over her head when I was around, and what with these rape charges floating around and everything I wasn't anxious to get caught looking. But the idea was for us all to go down there together, including Frankie Sullivan, and then as soon as Dede started to make her move, I would yell "Dogpile on Frankie" but I would *grab Dede* while she was all tangled up in her dress and push her down in the middle of the dogpile and do all the scientific research we needed before we let Frankie back up. I told Danny Bivens to make sure I had an extra fifteen or twenty seconds just for fumbling around with the metal support studs or whatever else Dede might have underneath there. It was perfect, cause the whole thing would look like an accident. I might have to say something to Miz Perryman like, "Yes, Ma'am, do I understand you to be saying that Dede

Wilks was trapped in some sort of unruly mob assembled on the Dwight D. Eisenhower Playground? Maybe you don't know it, Ma'am, but some of the older boys from the junior high have been wandering over here during the noon hour and if I were you I would do something about it before one of our girls gets seriously molested." But other than that, there was nothing that could go wrong with this plan.

We were luckier than we thought. When we got out to the Ike Playground, Dede Wilks was standing right next to the Climbing Tower, which was this steel treehouse where you were supposed to shimmy up one side and down the other, but what we mostly used it for was playing "Geronimo." I thought it was gonna take me forever to get Dede positioned between myself and Frankie Sullivan—let's face it, Frankie was getting a little paranoid by this time—but finally I did, and goldurn it if Dede didn't keep herself under control. She didn't even make a move for the dress.

With one eye on Frankie, who was kind of cowering behind the Dwight D. Eisenhower Parallel Pull-Up Device, I sidled up to Dede and said, "That certainly is a nice dress you have on today, Dede."

Dede got this grin on her face like a Methodist deacon that just ordered a Gin Fizz in Vegas. I saw her hand start moving down toward hem-level.

"I do believe it's one of the prettiest ones you've had on all week."

Damn if Dede didn't stop cold down by the poodle stitching when I said that.

"Course I wouldn't be intersted in *dresses.*"

She started up again. Sometimes you have to use reverse psychology on a bimbo like Dede.

Then she hesitated again. "Joe Bob, usually there aren't this many people around," she said.

"I know, Dede, wouldn't it be embarrassing if your dress was to fly up by accident and they all saw it?"

Dede nodded her head.

Something caught my attention out of the corner of my eye, and I swiveled around and saw about thirty guys standing *directly* behind me instead of lurking behind the Ike equipment like I told em to, and for just a minute I thought it was all over and I was about to yell at Danny Bivens for screwing everthing up, but then something else caught my attention and I saw this human blur heading toward the rope ladder and I thought it was Dede making a run for it and since I have the natural athletic instincts of a mountain lion I naturally broke in that direction myself so I could herd her back over to the Climbing Tower. But as soon as I took off for the blur, somebody yelled "Dogpile on Dede!" and I froze in my tracks and looked back over my shoulder just in time to see Dede with her dress thrown clean over her head and all thirty guys jumping on her at once, including five that did Geronimos off the tower.

I couldn't hardly believe it.

The human blur was Frankie Sullivan running like a crippled prairie dog, and I knew that as soon as he got to Miz Perryman it was all over.

By this time the dogpile was already about eight feet high and Dede was screaming for help and I stood there and yelled at Danny Bivens to break out of the pack and see if he couldn't bust it up, but he kept hollering back at me, "She won't let me, she won't let me."

So I reached down in the pile myself and started yanking out little guys, mostly second-graders, until one of em bit me on the elbow and I had to throw him back in. All this time Dede kept yelling "Rape! Rape!" and giggling a lot.

Now I don't know what you would of done, but when I

looked across the schoolyard and saw seven teachers and the principal and Frankie Sullivan coming our way, I decided to do all ten exercises on the Dwight D. Eisenhower Physical Fitness Playground obstacle course. I started with the Overhand Climb and got about halfway across before I heard the sound of Miz Perryman's voice.

"Joe Bob Briggs, what in tarnation is going on here?"

She grabbed me by the ear and yanked me down off the Overhand Climb and held me by both shoulders and started shaking me like a Raggedy Andy doll that's getting eat up by a pit bulldog. I could hardly talk for all the shaking she was doing, but I managed to get out, "What's going on here, Miz Perryman, is the fourth stage of the President Dwight D. Eisenhower Physical Fitness Course."

She slapped me up the side of the head three or four times. Then all the other teachers ran over to the Climbing Tower and started pulling people off the pile until they got to the bottom and found Dede down there, with her dress ripped clean off and a grin on her face like she just ate a toad sandwich.

Some people are animals.

One of the teachers—I think it was old Miz Hennessey—was the first to get to Dede and all she could say was, "The girl's been brutalized. This is terrible. Stand back, she's been through a trauma. Give her air, she's been brutalized."

And Dede never did say anything, she just kept the ignorant grin on her face, and so based on that they decided she was in a catatonic trance and they went and called the ambulance and some guys in white suits came and took her away, and all the time *that* was going on they had the thirty of us all herded into the Detention Hall, which made it pretty crowded in there since there was only five chairs. I went out in the hallway to complain

about the crowded conditions, but as soon as I stuck my
head out Miz Perryman liked to whacked it off with the
flat part of her hand so I come back inside.

"Well," I said to Danny Bivens, "I hope you got some
explanation."

"I don't know what come over me," said Danny. "I was
all ready to say 'Dogpile on Frankie,' but when she played
Big Top with her skirt, it came out 'Dogpile on Dede,' and
anyhow you waited too long because Frankie was already
halfway cross the schoolyard."

"Oh *yeah*, blame it on *me*, why don't you?"

"Well if you'd of took care of business at the drive-in in
the first place, we wouldn't of needed this plan at all."

"That's right, go ahead, make me the fall guy for the
stupidity of the entire school. That's okay, I'm used to it.
Don't worry about it. But I'll tell you one thing, Bivens,
the next time you come around to collect your 1 per cent
rake, you can *forget it*. Understand me? Handicappers are
a dime a dozen, and there's plenty of guys in the fifth
grade that'll do it for half the commission."

"Well I don't think there's gonna *be* any more commission, because Frankie told em everthing and this time I
think they're gonna believe him."

That was one I hadn't thought of, but I had no way of
knowing the kind of chicken manure that was coming our
way. First Miz Perryman whaled the tar out of about half
of us—she let the first- and second-graders go, *as usual*—
and then she sent us to the principal and we got stropped
again. The principal was this ninety-year-old junior-high
shop teacher named Mr. Vessle, and he wasn't happy just
to smack the fire out of us, he had to ask questions. Like,
"Just what did you boys think you were going to do to that
girl out there in the middle of the playground?"

Danny Bivens said, "I don't know."

"You don't know? You don't *know*?"

I've told Danny a thousand times never to say "I don't know" to a teacher cause that's the kind of reaction you always get.

"Well," said Mr. Vessle, "do you think if maybe I gave you fifteen or twenty more licks with this paddle then you would *know* next time?"

Danny said, "No, sir."

"What do you *mean,* 'No, sir'? Do you mean you'll *never* know the difference between right and wrong, or do you mean I need to hit you *more* than twenty times?"

Danny looked confused and didn't say nothing.

"I guess you don't have anything to say now, do you?" said Mr. Vessle.

"No, sir."

Sometimes I think Danny was born with ravioli for brains, cause he never *did* catch on to how all these conversations with the principal are fixed so they get you to say "No, sir" so then they can yell at you some more. So I figured I'd try to help Danny out.

"Mr. Vessle, if I could just have a moment of your time here, Sir, I'd like to point out . . ."

"Briggs, did I give you permission to talk?"

Now see what he's doing there? Danny would of fallen for that one, cause it was an obvious attempt to get me to say "No, sir" so he could hassle me some more. So I came back at him through the side door.

"I would prefer not to talk, sir, but I have some information that might clear all this up and let us get back to the educational process."

"Oh, you *do,* do you?"

"Yes, sir." (See, if you can get into a position of saying "Yes, sir," then you got him.)

"All right, Briggs, what is this information?"

"Well, first of all, I'd like to point out that I was not personally involved in the incident. I did happen to be in the vicinity, cause I was going through my daily workout on the President Dwight D. Eisenhower Physical Fitness Course."

"I didn't think anybody ever used that stuff."

"Oh yes, sir, some of us love the Ike equipment. It makes American youth strong."

"Okay, so what?"

"So I would just like to say that I saw most of the incident develop, and as an impartial witness I can say that Danny appeared to be trying to stop the fight and protect the girl's honor."

"Oh, you did?"

"Yes, sir." (You see how this goes once you take the bull by the horns?)

"Well, unfortunately for both of you guys, I'm afraid the matter is out of my hands. The parents have heard about this, and the girls' mothers are so upset that they're threatening to close the school unless we get some kind of explanation."

"Yes, sir," I said, "I can see how they'd want that, and they're *entitled* to an explanation."

I have to admit I was getting a little scared at this point.

"And you're going to *give* them an explanation. I want both of you at the gymnasium tomorrow night for the PTA meeting. All of the parents are coming, and they want answers."

Now I was ready to throw up.

I guess just about everybody in the county showed up at PTA that month, mainly cause deep down in their guts they wanted it to be true that there was a rape on the elementary-school playground. Sheriff Nogales came by the house the afternoon before the meeting that night to talk to my parents, and thank God Daddy wasn't home from the dirt mines yet.

"Miz Briggs," the Sheriff said, "it's our understanding

that a young girl got molested on the playground yesterday and that your boy might be involved in some way."

"Joe Bob?"

"Yes, Ma'am, we don't have all the pieces put together
yet, but evidently the Wilks girl went through quite a
psychological trauma and we'd preciate it if you'd have
your boy over at the school tonight."

"I will, Sheriff, but I'm sure Joe Bob's not mixed up in
anything like that."

At least my own mama trusted me.

Then after the Sheriff left, Mama kicked me from one
end of the house to the other end and kept hollering
"What the hell'd you do to that little girl?"

"Mama, she's not a *little* girl. Dede Wilks could bench-
press a water buffalo."

That's when Mama drew blood.

Things got worse at the actual meeting. First the principal got up and made a long boring speech about how the
school's ability to police the playground was severely
handicapped by the failure to pass the recent bond issue
and how blah blah blah educational process blah blah blah
strong minds and strong bodies blah blah blah emphasis
on discipline, both mental and physical blah blah blah
trying to fill in the pieces blah take measures to avoid
future incidents blah blah blah . . . and I thought he was
gonna go on forever until Scrim Wilks stood up in the
audience and said, "Well, did my little girl get diddled or
not?"

It can be durn scary when a room gets that quiet that
fast.

"I believe we have a witness present," said Miz Perryman, and she stood up and yanked this little kid up by the
shoulder and I about had a heart attack cause it was
Frankie Sullivan and I could see the memories of every
dogpile in history dancing through his brain. Frankie had

a blank expression on his face, like he didn't know exactly where he was.

"Well Frankie, go ahead," said Miz Perryman.

Frankie looked like he was gonna cry. He mumbled something but nobody could hear him.

"Frankie, you're going to have to speak up, honey."

"Joe Bob did it."

I guess when I heard that I was ready to pack my bags and head for the Huntsville State Prison, cause I knew I was gonna be the first nine-year-old kid in history to get the lectric chair.

"Joe Bob did what, honey?"

"Joe Bob and Danny."

At least I'd have a cellmate.

"Darling, you're going to have to tell us what Joe Bob and Danny did."

"Joe Bob and Danny made . . ."

"Yes, dear?"

"Joe Bob and Danny made a pile . . ."

For a second I thought Frankie wasn't gonna go through with it.

"Joe Bob and Danny made a pile on me."

Several of the mothers in the audience made loud gasps like they were gonna fall down dead, and Danny's daddy was in the back of the room and I could hear him saying, "That's the most disgusting thing I've every heard in my entire life."

Mr. Vessle was getting nervous, though, and so he turned off the microphone and went over to Miz Perryman and said, "What is this child talking about?" And Miz Perryman hesitated for a minute, and so he said, "That's what I thought. Now look, I don't want this pile being discussed any further at the PTA meeting, do you understand? We didn't come here to talk about a pile being deposited on this child."

"No sir, we didn't." (When I heard Miz Perryman say "No sir," I knew we had a chance.)

"Excuse me, Principal, I think I may be able to bring some light to bear on this." Old Miz Hennessey was asking for the floor.

"When I arrived at the scene," she said, "there were approximately two dozen boys rough-housing in the dirt with that poor girl. It appeared that they engaged in some kind of filthy sport."

"Can you be more specific?" said Vessle. "What do you mean 'sport'?"

"I conducted some very extensive questioning of one of the younger children involved, and I believe they were participating in some kind of wager."

Somebody stood up on the back row and screamed, *"I heard there's gambling in the elementary school!"*

This is what happens when they want to get you. You just start to get your good name cleared on one charge, and here they come after you on something else.

"My boy says the same thing." It was Mr. Shifton talking, and since Mr. Shifton only talks about once a year, everbody calmed down and listened to him.

"My boy didn't have nothin to eat for a whole week one time, and come to find out he was gamblin away all his lunch money."

This was an absolute lie if it's what Jimbo Shifton told his daddy, cause one thing I was always proud of was how, if you did binness with Joe Bob Briggs, you'd never go hungry. If you lost all your lunch money by morning reecess, I'd throw a complimentary lunch your way. I probly bought more free lunches than any kid in the history of elementary school.

The principal stood back up and said, "Did Jimbo say what type of gambling was involved, Mr. Shifton?"

But Mr. Shifton just said "Nope" and set back down.

"I know what type of gambling it was."

It seems like once something like this gets started, everbody wants to get in the act. This time it was Molly Ragsdale's mama.

"Molly says that most of the boys in her class have been wagering on one of the older girls."

"Which class would that be, ma'am?"

"Miz Perryman. I understand it's been going on for some time."

Vessle was getting nervous again, but what the heck could he do? "And what type of wagering did you say it was?"

"I understand they would give bets to the Briggs boy."

I knew what this meant. If the governor pardoned me and I got off on the rape charges, I was going to *federal* prison for running a gambling operation.

"Is that true, Joe Bob?"

Vessle was staring me down, like he thought for some reason *I* had the answers to all these controversies.

"Yes, sir, Mr. Vessle, I can't deny it."

"Do you realize what a serious offense gambling is?"

"Yes, sir, I do."

"And did you take all of Jimbo Shifton's money?"

"I don't see how that could be possible, sir, because all we were doing is pitching pennies. If my arithmetic is correct, Jimbo would have to lose 175 times in a row in order to lose all his lunch money for a week."

"Is that what you were doing? Pitching pennies?"

"Yes, sir, I do have to admit that we were. But with all due respect, sir, I think the matter of a possible sexual crime on the Dwight D. Eisenhower Physical Fitness Course is what should be occupying our attention at the present time."

"Oh you *do*, do you?"

"When are we gonna find out whether my girl got did-dled or not?" Scrim yelled.

"Wait just a minute!" It was Miz Ragsdale again. "Molly described the gambling as having something to do with the rape victim."

"Mrs. Ragsdale," said Vessle, "we're all anxious to find out what happened, but I do think 'rape' is a rather strong word at this point."

"The boys were betting money on the size of that girl's bust line."

Everbody was a little startled when Miz Ragsdale said that, including Vessle, who said, "What?"

"That's what Molly said."

"Mrs. Ragsdale," Vessle said, "I don't think this is some-thing we should be talking about at a public meeting unless it has some bearing on the alleged molestation."

"I'm just telling you what Molly said."

"All right." Vessle glared at me for a minute and I thought he was gonna ask me something, but he reconsid-ered and fixed on Danny.

"Danny Bivens, do you know anything about the Wilks girl?"

I could tell Danny was sweating this one, and I knew he was on the verge of saying "No, sir," and then Vessle would have him by the gazebos. Danny was all tore up inside and afraid of going to Huntsville with me and he thought everthing might be riding on this one answer. He cleared his throat two or three times.

"Yes, sir."

I couldn't believe it.

"And what *do* you know about the Wilks girl?" said Vessle.

"I know she has a . . . a glandular problem."

I don't guess I've ever been prouder of a person in my life than I was for Danny at that moment. As soon as he said "glandular," all the fathers started buzzing in the back, whispering to one another to try to find out what we were talking about. Vessle turned beet red. A few of the mothers gasped again. In the temporary confusion, I leaned over to Danny and grabbed him by the arm and said, "By the way, did you check em?"

Danny looked back at me and grinned. "We *all* checked em."

"I wanna know if my girl got diddled!"

Scrim Wilks was obviously gonna be our biggest obstacle to getting loose on this one.

"I agree with you, Mr. Wilks," said Vessle. "Now I think the best thing to do at this point is move away from this gambling issue entirely . . ."

Thank you, God.

". . . and address the molestation issue."

"It wasn't no molly-station."

At first I didn't recognize the voice, it come from so far away, but then everbody turned around and I turned with em and there in the back doorway of the gym was Dede Wilks. Here she was, ready to accuse me of rape in front of God, the school, and all Krankaway County.

"Excuse me," said Vessle, "but I thought we agreed the girl shouldn't be subjected to this."

"If she wants to talk," said Scrim, "let her talk."

"All right, Dede, why don't you walk down front so we can hear you."

Dede didn't just *walk* down front. Dede never just *walked* anywhere. The way Dede moved down to the front of the gym, she could of rewrote the Gettysburg Address with her rear end. When Dede finally turned around, I leaned over to Danny Bivens and said, "40DD+1C."

Vessle said, "What do you have to tell us, Dede?"

"I just wanted to say that I have a set of trick titties."

What I heard next was this sound that I never heard any time in my life before or since and I'll do my best to try to describe it. It was sort of like all the air being let out of the Goodyear Blimp at once so that it creates a complete vacuum and the world's biggest explosion at the same time. I can't remember whether it was the loudest room or the quietest room I've ever been in, and I wouldn't of known anyway cause Danny Bivens and me were down under our chairs rolling around with the veins sticking out on our heads and gasping for breath and trying to regain our vision and hearing. I would say it took about fifteen minutes to restore order to the room, and even then they had to put cold packs on Scrim Wilks so he wouldn't pass out again.

"Now Dede," Vessle finally said, "I want to ask you one question at a time and I don't want you to volunteer any further information. Is that clear?"

"Yes, sir," Dede said.

"Did anything happen to you on the playground yesterday?"

"Yes, sir."

"Please describe what happened."

I leaned over and told Danny I'd see him in Huntsville.

"Me and some of the boys exercised by the Climbing Tower."

"What do you mean by 'exercised'?"

"Exercise is what you do on the Dwight D. Eisenhower Physical Fitness Course."

Somewhere in heaven I saw a little light shine on my innocent head.

"But what *else* happened yesterday? Why were all of you on the ground, soiling your clothing?"

"Oh yeah, I forgot. Some people were doing Geronimos off the Climbing Tower and they knocked us down."

"Geronimos?"

"Yes, sir."

"And you're saying that all that happened is you got knocked down?"

"Yes, sir."

Vessle wasn't buying it.

"Now listen to me, Dede, I want you to tell us the exact truth and I want you to tell us *everything* you know about this. This is a very serious matter. Do you understand?"

"Yes, sir."

"All right. Do you know anything about wagering on your trick . . . wagering on your bust line?"

"No, sir."

"Now think very hard, Dede." Vessle stared over at me. "Think very hard about whether you've ever seen anyone taking money from other children when you were around."

"Well, there *was* one time, but I don't know what it means."

I knew she was laying for me, I just didn't know when it was coming.

"And when was that?"

"Almost every day Slopehead Frammolino would stand out . . ."

"Dede, are you speaking of Stephen Frammolino?"

"Yes, sir. Stephen Frammolino. Every day he would stand out on the road as I was coming in to school and he would stare at my bosoms, and then later I would see him get some money from the first-graders."

"Do you know the names of any of these first-graders?"

"Yes, sir. One of em was Jimbo Shifton."

I couldn't hardly believe it. Vessle was so happy to have a solution to the whole deal that he wrapped it up in about five minutes after that. Then when Dede was leaving, she looked right at me as she passed and I stared back at her and said, "Hey, Dede, see you at the drive-in."

Dede turned red, and I said, "No charge."

Then Scrim came and got her and I turned and looked at Danny Bivens and said, "You know, I could marry that girl some day."

Slopehead Frammolino got expelled for gambling at school, which just goes to prove a great truth about this country of ours, which is:

Education is our greatest asset, but some people squander it through their own immaturity.

3

Interruption to Explain Why You Should Never Get Married in West Texas

Since we're evidently gonna be talking about my personal life for a while, I think it might be a good time to start clearin up some of the vicious rumors that were spread about the area of Texas where I grew up, specially the one about geography, geology, history, and distribution of Wal-Mart shoppin centers out there. I grew up in what you call your Panhandle. Now there's two Panhandles. There's the Oklahoma Panhandle, which looks just exactly like a moon crater except for the town of Guymon, which looks like the white part of a Band-Aid after it's been on your knee for six days. And then there's the Texas Panhandle, which looks like a plastic Bugs Bunny plate with some leftover green beans on it. There's one green bean on the bottom part. That's Lubbock. And there's one green bean up on the top part. That's Amarillo. And then somewhere in the middle, but closer to the top green bean, there's a crack in Bugs's left paw. That's the Palo Duro Canyon, where millions of tourists come ever year to ride baby burros and see the outdoor historical pageant "Erastus." It's about the famous deaf-mute hero of the Texas Revolution who founded Erastus County and never did learn sign language. It's a musical, with teenage volunteer Vegas lounge singers in white shoes livin there for the summer and takin parts in the production and runnin around in designer cowboy hats singin songs like "Drivin Them Cattle On Home" and "Brandin Time" and "He Cain't Talk, He's a Mute." If you're ever in the area, it's well worth takin your whole family to see it, specially if you have relatives intersted in feedlot history.

Okay, now if you'll just follow this map on down Bugs's elbow, the one that sticks out from his hip when he's mad, you'll get to the approximate location of Krankaway County. It's shaped like this:

A lot of times you'll notice the shape of Krankaway County printed on T-shirts or cardboard boxes, identifyin the product as comin from our part of the country. We applied for a copyright on the shape about twenty years ago, but it never has come through.

There's two big towns in the county. Bison, the county seat, would be about 10 o'clock on Mickey's little hand, and Frontage Road would be 3:30 on the big hand. Halfway between Bison and Frontage Road is the school district town, which is called "The School," and basically all we got there is a football stadium and some brick buildins and about 118 school buses all lined up on the asphalt lot.

We got about 4,000 people in the county. We got 17,000 cattle most years, 28,000 rattlesnakes, 57,000 tumbleweeds, and 128,000 Babtist churches. We have one tree. Jerry Meyers trucked it in from Alamogordo. It's a muskberry tree. One year it bore fruit, and Jerry's eight-year-old ended up gettin sent away to the State Mental Reetard School for the Feeble-Minded in Denton cause he ate a bunch of muskberries one day and forgot all his multiplication tables except nine times twelve.

What we ain't got is women.

Since this is gonna be the basic topic of the whole rest of this book, I imagine I better explain. I didn't say we don't got *females.* We got plenty of them. But we only got three basic types:

1. Baby mushmouth Gerber-spitters. (And while I'm on the subject, would you people with nickel cameras please *stop* takin pictures of babies eatin, we're sick of it, okay? It's not somethin mankind wants to see.)

2. Beanstalk Jailbait. (Girls like Dede Wilks, dumb as a bag of ball bearings.)

3. Women With Thighs the Size of Libya. (This is 98 per cent of the female population.)

Now let's discuss the prospects for a guy like my own-self. We do have a *slight* chance for eternal happiness in Krankaway County. There's a period of about *two weeks* in a Krankaway County girl's life where you can bear the thought of takin one home to your trailer house. It happens when they turn 17, 18, around in there. (I'm only talkin about *some* of em now. There's some Krankaway County girls that we use for fireplace pokers beginning at age nine, they're so ugly.) Anyhow, there's this two weeks where they lose all their acne, they grow boobs, they have most of their teeth, and they weigh less than 230 pounds. If you're *real* quick, and you have the ability to predict just exactly which girl will become humanoid during which year, then you can try to grab em and marry em before they start lookin like helium balloons with leprosy again.

Here's the part you don't know, though. A lot of these

Krankaway County girls spend the summer between their junior and senior year of high school at the Miss Texas Pageant Charm School, Dance Academy, and Institute of Incredible Cosmetic Lies. It costs you 200 bucks a week, includin room and board at the Miss Texas world headquarters in Fort Worth. And so they come back from Fort Worth *planning* on this two weeks of their lives where they're gonna get you to buy em a ring and a trailer, fertilize em a while so they can domino two or three yard monsters, and then retire to the Piggly Wiggly frozen food department, where they can grow some titanic hineys, wear white shorts that leave permanent rings on their thunder thighs, make thwackin noises everwhere they go from their thongs flappin against their heels, and cut off all their hair like Anne Murray. You see? Before you know what's happenin, they've moved from Beanstalk Jailbait to Bimbo with Thighs the Size of Libya, and *you're married to one of em*. Not only that, they have three little Frito-eatin tax deductions that are worth $750 each *per month* if you ever get the insane idea of packin your fishin gear and headin for Lake of the Ozarks to live with an alligator gar for a while.

In other words, you are in a no-win situation.

This is just to explain why I admired Dede Wilks for her mind, and *not* for her body. Bodies come and go. Women that'll lie to the principal for you are worth waitin on.

I probly would of married her, right then and there, but I got saved first.

I'm gonna need a whole nother chapter for that story.

4

A Bunch of Jesus Stuff

I'm afraid I'm gonna have to ask you to repent from your sins now.

I know it's not easy. I know we're only up to Chapter 4 and so far there's nothing in this book about drive-ins or the history of the world or nekkid women, except for Dede Wilks who don't count, and here I go turning religious on you. So go on ahead and throw the book out if you want to. I'm not gonna stop you. I'll understand. I don't care if you wanna throw Jesus down the old toilet bowl, it don't mean diddly to me. I'll pray a little for you, do what I can, but I'm afraid the Big Guy is gonna be a little p.o.ed. *And you know what He does when He gets mad?* Huh? Do you?

He gets another talk show on cable.

What I'm trying to say is, there comes a time when a man's got to change his ways. I wanna get serious here for a moment, cause this is not the time to take this book lightly. I'm about to give my testimony to the nations, and if the nations aren't listening, I guess I'll have to give it to the dimwits that bought this book, but either way it's confession time. Assume an attitude of *reverence*, if you would. I don't want any of you guys in Jersey thinking you can skip to the next chapter or anything like that, because

the time is now. This is life and death. There is no tomorrow. Okay. That's better. Now.

Let's talk about the J-Man.

I got saved in 1958, one weekend around Easter when I
was cruising Federal Highway 84, searching for spiritual
knowledge. Actually what I was searching for was a girl
named Ginny Pounders, who had a habit of standing
around in front of the Dary Queen and saying stuff like, "I
don't know, how nasty do you think I am?" Ever once in a
while Buster Dary would come out and run her off his
gravel lot, but usually Buster just left her alone as long as
she didn't scare off business or start making "Cherry
Coke" jokes. I liked Buster. Buster used to be named
Virgil Smith, but he went down to the Krankaway County
Courthouse and told the judge how people always made
fun of him for having the name "Smith," and he wanted it
changed to Buster Dary, and then it was right after that
he opened the Dary Queen. Buster used to get sued about
97 times a year by the Dairy Queens International, who
said there was a resemblance between the name Buster
Dary and the name Dairy Queen, but I never could see
the connection. What did they want him to do, call it the
Buster Queen?

Anyhow, if you gave Ginny Pounders five dollars, sometimes she'd turn her pelvis into a human milk-shake machine. (If you're referrin to the categories in the last chapter, Ginny Pounders was a fairly prime cut of Beanstalk
Jailbait, but when you grow up in Krankaway County,
anything that can balance on high heels and face forward
when it walks is considered worthy of attack.)

But on this night I'm talking about, I couldn't find
Ginny Pounders and so I started looking for spiritual
knowledge. Actually what I was looking for was some
Vision Beer, cause I didn't wanta drive way the heck over
to New Mexico for a shipment but I still felt like puking

my guts out a little bit that night. So I tooled on down 84 to
the Valhalla Drive-In, the same place where Dede Wilks
raped me, and escaped prosecution for child abuse because, at the time, I didn't know how to nail her on that
rap. But I was sick of Dede and her trick titties by this
time, and so I nosed into a space next to Bobo Rodriguez
during the scene where the blood-drinking Martian monster starts sucking astronauts to death in *It! The Terror
from Beyond Space.* Bobo was not amused. Bobo was
never very good at science, so the only flicks he liked at
the drive-in were the ones that had Jerry Lewis acting like
a drunk reetard. Bobo used to talk about how he liked
"the early Jerry" a lot better than "the late Jerry." The
late Jerry was the years when Jerry cut way back on the
number of times he'd jump around pigeon-toed, dance
with a mop, and say *"Ahyoogilvimble!"* in any one given
movie. Bobo'd seen all the Jerry movies about 38 times
each, and you could never disturb him when he was
watching one of em, cause all he'd ever do is stare at the
screen and once in a while he'd say, "Take a hike, Dino."
That's all: "Take a hike, Dino." And then he'd turn quiet
again. So when I nosed into the space next to Bobo, I
checked the screen first to make sure it wasn't a Jerry
flick, then I sat there till the part where Crash Corrigan
starts ripping through the metal with his claws and then I
got out and invited Bobo to come over and have a few
Visions in my Bel Air.

Before I tell you what happened next, to change the
whole history of the universe, I got to tell you about Bobo.

Bobo Rodriguez became my best friend in Frontage
Road, even if he did forget what race he was a lot. Bobo
was about six-foot-six and weighed about 230 and was so
strong he could kill a wild boar with his bare hands. I
know this because Bobo killed the only wild boar in
Krankaway County, and after he did it I said, "Bobo, that

really wasn't necessary, now was it, cause what are we gonna do with a dead wild boar?" But he was real proud of himself and wanted to put it up on the wall of his Pawnee shack. I talked him out of that, cause it was already too crowded in there for all Bobo's cousins to find a place to sleep, and so I carried it over to Mr. Godbey, thinking his science class might wanta stuff it or something, and Mr. Godbey turned Bobo in for destroying an endangered species. The federal government was supposed to make Bobo pay a thousand bucks, but when they went out to Pawnee Town to serve him with the fine, Bobo was out in the front yard with his shirt off trimming his weeds and humming the drum solo to "Inna Gadda Divida," and they just said forget it. Bobo never did forgive me, though, cause the FBI kept his wild boar for evidence.

Bobo was older and bigger and stupider than I was, and so he taught me a lot of things about the meaning of life. One thing he taught me was to stop treating women like old pieces of dirty laundry and start treating em like pieces of discount furniture.

I'm bringing this up because Bobo's favorite thing in life to do was go to border towns. Bobo could find border towns in places where most people couldn't find borders. One time Bobo took me to a border town called Guerrero that was so little, when you asked where Boys Town was, they'd point to this old woman that had rubber teeth. To Bobo's credit, he didn't say "How much?" What he said was *"Cuánto?"* Normally the only thing Bobo says in a border town is *"Cuánto?"* Partly this is cause *"cuánto"* is the only word Bob knows in the Meskin language besides "Mesko."

Anyhow, I owe it to Bobo Rodriguez for getting me out of Frontage Road for the first time in my life. I was fourteen and Bobo said something like, "We go humpa-humpa in Boys Town?" And I thought Bobo was talking about Cal

Farley's Boys Ranch, where they take these disturbed youths of America and make em milk cows for seven years until they're bored into correct social behavior, and I said to Bobo "No way, José," cause ever since we got this new evangelist preacher named Cargile in town, saving people left and right down at Cavalry Babtist, they'd all been trying to stick me in Cal Farley's Boys Ranch, probly hoping I'd get trampled on by horses or wildebeests or something.

But it was a good thing for me that, soon as I said the word "José," Bobo assumed I spoke Meskin, and so the next thing I knew he was firing up the Pawnee Wagon. The Pawnee Wagon used to be a school bus, but Bobo stripped all the yellow paint off to give it that original structural-steel look, and then he hung straw curtains in all the windows so the ninety-two members of Bobo's family could have privacy when they were on family outings. He also put a brand-new tractor motor up front on the same night that H. M. Stiles reported part of his brand-new tractor missing, but I don't think there was any truth to the rumors that the two events were related. The Pawnee Wagon could top out at about 27 on the interstate. It took Bobo about as long to get out of town as it's taking me to tell this story.

What I'm getting to is this: Bobo was one of those guys who got in fights more than most people got insulted. Sometimes Bobo would of had three fights before he ate breakfast, but what I like about Bobo was he only had fights over things that mattered. Like whether you're supposed to turn in a W-2 form when you drive a school bus. Like whether Yoakum County is bigger than Krankaway County. Like whether he did or didn't say "Excuse me" when he bumped into Dumptruck Lewis's wife while they were going through the automatic door at Boyle's Market. That one was bound to turn into a fight, since

Dumptruck Lewis used to fight as much as Bobo. At least Dumptruck had an excuse, though, cause ever since he came back from Ko Rea he got radio messages on the metal plate in his head. One of the messages told him to go get married to Maxine "Doorknob" Slatts, so we knew he was capable of just about anything.

You're probly wondering why I'm telling you all this. I don't have any idea. Oh, yeah.

So when I went over to Bobo's car that night, right in the middle of *It! The Terror from Beyond Space*, Bobo saw me out of the corner of his eye, rammed his fist through the plate glass on his passenger window, grabbed me by the collar, and jerked me into his front seat hoping I was Dumptruck Lewis. But when he saw it was only me, he said, "We go humpa-humpa in Boys Town?"

That's the kind of guy Bobo was.

But I told him, no, I was just there to pick up a couple cases of Vision Beer, and he was welcome to help drink it in the Bel Air so long as he didn't start opening the cans with his teeth, Pawnee-style, and spraying foam all over the upholstery. So, to make a long story short, Bobo ended up parking his carcass in my car by the time the next feature started, which was *Jail Bait* (original 1955 version with Lyle Talbot and Steve Reeves before he got famous). Bobo kept asking me if Jerry was gonna be in it. I think that was when we started searching for spiritual knowledge.

Now I don't know how much you know about Vision Beer Number Four, but it's the only beer in the United States that's brewed out of cactus juice, the way the Indians used to make it. (I'm talking abut the *real* illegal Vision Beer now, the ones that cost ten cents a can, and not the three-twos they sold to tourists.) There's several kinds of it, but the only decent kick comes from the cactus they grow over at Elephant Butte Indian Reservation by Truth

or Consequences, New Mexico. Sometimes they'll try to
slip in some synthetic cactus juice that they make over in
Hobbs, but when that happens Vision Beer is the only
beer in the United States that can be chewed.

"Bobo," I said, "Are we talking Elephant tonight?"

Bobo looked straight at me, tried to focus in, his eyes
glazed over, and then he said, "Take a hike, Dino."

The stuff was already kicking in.

Right then I knew we were goners.

You remember the psychedelic kinescope sequence in
Hallucination Generation? How about when Bruce Dern
looks at Peter Fonda and says "Trust me" in *The Trip*?
How about the scene in *The Naked Zoo* where Rita
Hayworth starts freaking out? Remember when Wolf
Ruvinskis, the Meskin wrestler with lightning bolts on his
mask, tried to put a hammer-lock on a monster blood-
eating brain in *Neutron Against the Death Robots*? Remember when Wayne Newton took his shirt off in public?

Well, none of that stuff is half as scary as the eight-hour
descent into Hell with Bobo Rodriguez. Sometime while
we were still downing Vision Beers, the third feature
came on—*Devil Girl from Mars*, the classic about an
outer-space bimbo who rockets down to Earth to capture
men for breeding—and all of a sudden I thought of Dede
Wilks and I started to lose it. Everything got all mixed up.
I was being raped at the Dary Queen by Anne Francis in
Forbidden Planet, only she had zits on her face and she
kept saying, "Take a hike, Wino," while Danny Bivens
tried to make a dogpile on her and then Miz Perryman
started covering me up with Consolidated dirt and hosing
me down so everthing turned to mud and then Ginny
Pounders stood there and said "Nasty! Nasty! *You're*
nasty!" and then Bobo Rodriguez skidded on the mud and
lost control of his school bus and seventeen cousins were
flung in the air like the flying heads in *Night of the Blood*

Beast and then the next thing I knew Bobo was taking the steel plate out of Dumptruck Lewis's head and all this gooey stuff was coming out with it and all Bobo could say was *"Now we go humpty-dumpty-humpa."*

I looked over at Bobo and his eyes were glued to the screen. He thought he was watching a Jerry Lewis movie.

I don't know how long it went on—six, seven, eight hours maybe—and I thought I was making my last trip to Disneyland. I saw visions of the future, including every Yvonne De Carlo movie ever made, even the ones filmed in Italy by Carlo Ponti before he got fat. Then the Bel Air started to cave in on me, and Bobo Rodriguez started to pound me over the head with my own customized fuzzy dice, and the only thing that saved me was Dorothy Malone smothering me in her bazoomas in an attempt to keep the flying tarantula-men from eating off my face.

Then, gradually, I started hearing voices outside the car.

Deliver us JEEEE-ZUS . . . fiery destruction . . .

. . . and I kind of recognized it as the voice of Cargile, the new Babtist preacher in town, but I was still seeing Yvonne De Carlo all mixed up in there with Bobo Rodriguez and *Untamed Women,* which must of come on the screen around 4 in the morning and is pretty much the story of my life.

Fire from Heaven will BURN this place, thee and thou and I and we, and the babes and the righteous will walk through the flame and . . .

. . . and I started to remember this old flick called *The Unknown Terror,* where a mad scientist starts turning people into monsters covered with foam rubber and they don't know *what* the heck is happening except they'd probly walk through the flame, too, if they could excape the movie.

Do you SEE yonder shining light? It has life but we have death. Death. Death.

"Jesus Christ!" I finally said and sat straight up on my new polyethylene seat covers and stared out the front of my shatterproof windshield—and I'll be damned if it *wasn't* old Cargile, standing up on the merry-go-round in front of the drive-in screen while the morning sun rose up over the top of it behind him. Actually, I won't be damned if it wasn't him, cause that was gonna be the morning I was saved, so I can't be damned even if I say I'll be damned. You'll understand this once you finish reading this chapter and get yourself saved.

Anyhow, Cargile kept talking about Jesus—only he called it "JEEEEE-zus"—and life and death and shining lights and crowns of glory, and pretty soon I started wondering where the heck I was, cause the last thing I remembered I was trolling Highway 84, looking for Ginny Pounders, and now it was Sunday morning and some guy was up there threatening to burn down the drive-in. So I did what you always do at the drive-in when you don't know what the heck is going on. I laid on my horn as hard as I could, let that sucker blare out until old Cargile quit waving his arms around for a minute and looked square at me. And then I panicked again. I stared all around me, leaned over into the backseat and looked on the floor, threw 70 or 80 Vision Beer cans out the window so I could do a complete search, and then jumped out of the car and started screaming at Cargile.

"Where the heck is Bobo Rodriguez, you old fart!"

I think that was about the time I saw the *other* 900 cars parked at the drive-in.

Den of Iniquity, a Vehicular Sodom, Coughing Up Its Refuse.

I believe old Cargile was referring to my Vision Beer can collection, but I don't know.

Repent, I charge you! You! Joe Bob Briggs! Walk the aisle today. Dedicate your life. ACCEPT your salvation!

"I bet you repented Bobo Rodriguez right into the jailhouse, didn't you, Cargile?"

Heaven is waiting. Now. Today. Bring your sins to me, they are washed away—

I kinda liked that part of it, the part about your sins being washed away, but I didn't want Cargile *touching* my sins, even if he was promising to wash em, dry em, dry-clean em, and Simonize em. They were *my* goldurn sins and if I wanted to I'd buy em bolo ties and give em guest spots on *I Love Lucy*.

"Cargile, you know what? If I don't see Bobo Rodriguez in five minutes . . ."

Ask and ye shall receive. Seek and ye shall find. Knock and the door shall be opened to ye.

"Ye have four minutes now, before I turn ye face into yelly."

Woe to the sinner who lags behind! To the tardy comes damnation! To the lazy comes judgment! Repent now! Look about you! You're lost!

I don't know what it was about that last exclamation point, but it's the one that got to me. I looked around me and, dadburn it, I *was* lost. I looked down at my feet and I couldn't even see the toes on my imitation cowhide boots cause I was standing in a big heap of empty Vision cans and some Dr Pepper cups and corny-dog wrappers that were all mashed up together like a drive-in tumbleweed. I looked at my shirt and all I could see was a yellow glob of Mister Mustard and a belly button. I looked at my face but I didn't see nothing. I looked at my car and it looked like a couple hippopotamuses tried to have sex in there. I looked over at the driveway sign and it said "Valhalla Drive-In" in big letters, and then down on the bottom it had little plastic ones that said:

Easter Sunrise
Services
6:00 Drive-In Jesus Is Lord

And it was at *exactly* that moment, when I saw those
words up there on the marquee, it was right then I started
to shake so hard that the Vision cans flew up all around my
armpits and the people that had Cadillacs started getting
out and staring at me so I wouldn't blow dust over on em
and pretty soon my face started to twitch and I started
shouting out stuff like "Good golly, Miss Molly!"

And when I said that the congregation said "Amen!"

And then my left arm started jerking up and down like
a guy that's all wired up for brain research, so I said "Great
balls of fire!"

"Amen!"

Then my ears started flapping forward and backwards,
which is not something I normally do in front of strangers.
"One o'clock two o'clock three o'clock rock!"

"Amen!"

"Drive-In Jesus Is Lord!"

And when I said that, all of a sudden I heard this huge
sound like a sperm whale making love to a Hoover vac-
uum-cleaner factory, and I turned around and threw my
body down on the ground like a Fudgsicle that fell off the
little wooden stick. As soon as I did, my Bel Air rose
straight up in the air, and all the women started screaming to have mercy on em and then I saw Bobo Rodriguez,
standing there with his hands on the axle, dead-lifting that
car like Steve Reeves in *Hercules,* only he had this expression on his face like a deer on the first day of season. I
oughta explain right here that sometimes Vision Beer can
kick in twelve, fourteen hours after you first drink the
stuff and if you get that delayed reaction you either think
you're Steve Reeves or Buckwheat. It's a good thing Bobo

thought he was Steve Reeves, cause if he'd woke up thinking he was Buckwheat, he would of been one squashed Pawnee. But since he thought he was Steve Reeves, he looked like a miraculous vision. To this day there's Pawnee families all over Texas that have little clay statues sitting on top of their TV sets of a fat guy holding up a Bel Air. There's even a town down in Mexico where the Catholic church started worshipping "Saint Bobo" and teaching their children how to put hydraulic lifts on the fronts of their cars so they can make em do "The Bobo Miracle." Ever Sunday they go and light a candle at the tiny Bel Air Chapel, where they kneel quietly, cross themselves, sacrifice a wild boar, and chant "Humpa humpa" three times. I heard the Pope don't like it, but he didn't see the heft on that chassis when Bobo went religious on us.

"Drive-In Jesus Is Lord!" I said again, and this time all the people answered back, making a noise unto the Lord.

They all shouted, "What the heck you doing, Joe Bob?"

"Hosanna Banana, we have seen the resurrection!" I yelled. "Bobo lives! The Bel Air has risen! It's time!"

And they all shouted again. They shouted, "Whah?"

And then I got hysterical and started speaking in tongues.

"José can you see? Frera Jocka Dormay Voo! Gezundheit! Let's twist again!"

I was obviously out of control when I started doing reverse back flips off the high board *without a high board.* About three hundred people got personally concerned for my safety and swarmed over me and started giving me fist-to-mouth resuscitation until I passed out completely and they carried me out to the squad car so that I wouldn't get ripped to smithereens by individuals seeking spiritual knowledge and change for a five. The last thing I remember is clawing my way back up to the window and staring out at Cargile, who was so ticked off his pompadour was coming unglued. Cargile was looking at me and repeating the same words over and over again. I couldn't hear him through the glass, but I could see his lips moving.

"Fur Cue!"

I didn't know what he meant at the time. He just kept saying it. "Fur Cue! Fur Cue!" And it wasn't till years later, when I was hustling pool one night in Gallup, that I figured it out. There was this guy from Cheyenne showed up with a little fuzzy ball hanging off the back end of his pool cue, and he said, "I'm laying five-to-one on three-game eight-ball, plus five bucks a ball." Normally this was my kind of bet, but soon as I opened my mouth to say "Double the stake and go to fifteen and I'm ready to wrap your behind in a frozen-dinner plate," I went mute and I *remembered* the words the Reverend Cargile, my Babtist brother, said to me that morning. "Fur Cue!" It was a prophecy, a warning. That little ball hanging off the end of the guy's cue was *furry*. So I passed on the bet, and Cheyenne played a guy from Tucson and took him for 230. Which just goes to show, God wants me to be rich.

All I was trying to say in this chapter is how I was saved that day—April 27, 1958—and ever since then I been preaching the drive-in gospel and forgiving myself for all my sins, specially the ones that start with the letter "B." Think I'll go commit one right now, just to be safe.

5

Where the *Real* Book Starts

The first thing God did for me is He bought me a car. I would of been happy to keep driving that piece-a-crap Bel Air, but God commanded me to go find a '49 Mercury two-door coupe with less than 15,000 miles on it so I could lead my people out of Frontage Road. It made sense cause the Bel Air needed an alignment job after Bobo dumped it on the gravel and became Saint Bobo. If I'd known what a commotion it was gonna cause down in Mexico, I would of carved it up into 9,000 pieces and sold em off as religious relics to all the people who can't afford food so they buy religious relics instead. But God didn't direct me to become a millionaire at that particular point in my life. So I headed on down to Sal's-Vage Yard, which used to be Sal's Salvage Yard before Sal thought it was funny to call it "Sal's-Vage Yard," which might give you some idea of how many face cards were missing from Sal's deck, and when I pulled up Sal was just crawling out from underneath a burnt-out chassis that looked like something left over from *Hot Car Girl,* which was the second feature with *Cry Baby Killer,* which was Jack Nicholson's best performance before he started making indoor bullstuff on us.

And I said, "Sal, in the name of the Drive-In I command you to give me a '49 Mercury two-door coupe with less than 15,000 miles on it so I can lead my people out of Frontage Road."

And Sal said, "Okay."

And I was about to tell Sal how white he was for doing that, but then he said, "In the name of the Dollar I command you to give me 500 bucks."

And I said, "Sal, I'm sure we can work out some long-term financing if you got the car I need."

Sal got a grin on his face like he just ate a manure sandwich and a Twinkie. He turned around and motioned for me to follow him and then he walked about nine miles to the other end of the Sal's-Vage Yard, and then he rooted around behind some old sheets of tin and pushed em over on a '36 Ford that only had three wheels and then he ripped a Navaho blanket off the roof of a car and . . .

Excuse me just a minute while I get my breath.

And There It Was.

It was at sunset when I first laid eyes on it, so it looked like it was rising up out of a pillar of fire, or maybe it looked like the upholstery was on fire, or maybe it just looked like it got burned up in a fire one time, but anyhow it was the most beautiful four-wheeled motor vehicle in the history of civilization.

It was a 1949 Mercury two-door coupe, chopped, channelled, and lowered, with teardrop spots on each side, the grille from a '53 Chevy welded on with extra teeth for shark-tooth effect, three-bar Fiesta spinners on the front wheels, cruiser skirts on the back, rolled and pleated leather interior, angel hair in the back window, chrome-tubing organ-pipe AM speakers with automatic fader, and —get this—it was painted my favorite color: Tahitian Red. When you turned the key in the ignition, it played the Hallelujah Chorus.

"Sal," I said, "God put this car here for me."

"Yeah, I know," Sal said, "and God told me you'd be bringing 500 bucks when you picked it up."

"Sal, you ever heard of thirty-year financing?"

"What?"

"They do it all the time now, specially preachers. I put up a big down payment, something in the high single digits, and you get a payment ever three months for the rest of your life."

"Yeah?"

"Yeah, they call it thirty-year financing, but you can really get it for as long as you want. I'd prefer not to go more than thirty, but if you want forty, fifty, I might give it to you as a friend. But I can't go more than fifty, I'm sorry, it just wouldn't be Christian."

"Yeah?"

"Sal, I notice that's the second time you've said 'Yeah.' "

"Yeah?"

"Sal, can I be frank with you?"

"Yeah?"

"Sal, I'm no salesman. I can't make you sell me this car if you don't want to sell me this car. I can't even make you *give* me this car. But what we're talking about here is the Divine Will, now do you know what this is?"

"Yeah?"

"No, you don't, Sal, you do not know what that is, otherwise you wouldn't be standing here arguing with me about the financing terms on a car that God has ordered me to drive out of Frontage Road, Texas, so that the history of the world can continue. Now do you understand me?"

"Yeah?"

"I thought so. Now Sal, I want you to pray with me right now. I want you to put your hands on the hood ornament and pray over this motor vehicle with me. And as we do that, I want you to find it in your conscience to do the right thing and hand me over the keys and trust in God to make the payments. Sal, would you demand money from God?"

Sal didn't answer right off.

"Of course, you wouldn't. But it's a good thing for you, Sal, that God has decided to buy this car for me, cause that means you'll be getting the payments direct from the Home Office. Now listen to me, Sal. No repo problems, right, cause how you gonna repo a car from God?"

"Yeah?"

"That's better. They don't have no wreckers in heaven, do they, Sal?"

Sal seemed to be struggling with himself inside, and I could see the Holy Drive-In Word was starting to have an effect on him.

"No, Sal, they don't have no wreckers in heaven, cause they don't have no wrecks, they don't have no repo men, they don't have no speed limits."

Sal shut his eyes and started shaking.

"No, Sal, they don't have no speed limits in heaven!"

"Yeah!"

"That's right, and so what you gonna do, Sal? What you gonna do now?"

"Yeah!"

"I know, Sal, but tell me. What you gonna do with the car?"

"Yeah!"

"Yeah and Amen, I know, but I *need* the Mercury. It's not even me that needs it, but it's the Drive-In Jesus that needs that Merc. And you're gonna give it to me, aren't you?"

"Yeah!"

And as soon as he said that, I took off running and jumped in the front seat and fired her up and smashed through a Dr Pepper sign and ran over a toolbox before I

got her out to the highway and pretty much left Sal chok-
ing blue smoke.

Even after Sal sued me, in direct violation of his verbal
agreement, I prayed thanks to the Lord ever night for
giving me that Mercury and making people like Sal possible, cause without me, people like me would need money
all the time. This is why it says in the Bible "blessed are
the poor and the ones that know how to turn bullshit into
a free meal."

6

The Years of Persecution, or At Least a Coupla Days of It

Once you get saved, you got to talk to God all the time. I didn't count on this part of it. For the first couple years I'd start in talking to God ever night before I went to bed, but I kept slipping in the f-word before I could help myself, and then I'd have to apologize to the Guy for about two hours before I figured I was sorry enough and so I could go on to bed. Then I tried talking to God without moving my lips, but I kept biting my tongue. So after a while I just broke clean off, looked up at Him, and said, "Hell, we ain't got nothin to talk about anyhow," and He didn't fry my feet off or turn me into a Pentecostal or nothing so I imagine He agreed with me. I did ask the Big Guy to send me some more visions, though, and He delivered on those mothers.

About all I did after I got saved was go to the drive-in and hang around the concession stand and tell people how Drive-In Jesus Is Lord. Then, after I got kicked out, I'd go over to Lubbock and look for some demons to fight off. It was Bobo that first told me how the demons work and how you got to mash em up like sweet potatoes so you can puke em out and get rid of em. This was later proved up by the drive-in classic *The Exorcist,* but as you can see, Bobo was a man a way ahead of his time.

Once you start thinking about this bullstuff, you got

demons all over the lot. Like one time Bobo come over to the house and he said, "Joe Bob, my head crooked." That's all he said, just like that. "Joe Bob, my head crooked."

So I said, "What part of your head's crooked, Bobo?"

And Bobo said, "Don't know, cause head crooked."

Sometimes Bobo could be one smartass Pawnee if you didn't watch him, so I walked all around him before I answered back. I stared at the back of his head, and it looked normal, like somebody busted a can of Raviolios over his skull. And then I walked around to the side and stared at his ears, and they looked normal, except for the place where Bobo burned all his hair off the night he was showing the Boy Scout troop the ancient Pawnee ritual of the flaming gearshift knob. And finally I went around front and looked straight in Bobo's face, and his eyes looked like they were stapled together and mailed off parcel post to Cleveland. And I knew right then what was wrong, but I wanted to be sure, so I said, "Bobo, you always been this ugly?"

And he said, "I think for about twenty-six years."

And I calculated that was about right, since Bobo was twenty-four years old. So I said, "In that case, Bobo, you have a demon in your face."

And Bobo started to get mad, cause he thought I was talking about his "race" instead of his "face," and I had to explain to him that it didn't have a thing to do with his family, it was just a plain simple fact that he was possessed by a little slimy devil and it probly explained a whole lot about why he looked like he just crawled up out of a Dempster Dumpster and, besides, if we just prayed a little bit and bashed Bobo's face in with a dirty tennis shoe, we could run that little bastard out of there in five minutes. Bobo looked happy when I told him that, but he didn't smile, cause apparently the demon was working his way down to the lip area, trying to make Bobo look like the monster in *Orlak, El Infierno de Frankenstein,* the 1960 Meskin classic about the creature that gets his face melted down so they have to do the whole movie with a steel box on his head.

"Bobo, if this demon does much more damage, we're gonna have to build a permanent No. 10 two-ply Safeway bag around your head."

And evidently the demon heard me say that, cause he started making a noise like a TV evangelist filling out his internal-revenue forms, and it sounded like he was gonna do something drastic, like give Bobo acne inside his nose, and so I started screaming for the Drive-In Jesus to *heal* this Bobo and *fry* this man's brain till that demon *begged* for mercy Amen! and it was one of them *ugly ugly pure dee ugly demons* Amen! and maybe if we could smoke it out Bobo could get a *date* with a human bean Amen! and soon as I said that Bobo let out a big breath of air and he said, "There is nothing wrong with me at this time, Mr. Briggs."

And of course I was all caught up in burning up Bobo's demon and so I said, "What?"

And Bobo said, "I am a healed individual."

And, I don't know, but it didn't seem like Bobo to me, specially since he sounded exactly like Conway Twitty in *Platinum High School.*

"Bobo, do you realize you're talking like Conway Twitty?"

Bobo didn't say nothing, so I figured the demon didn't wanna give hisself away.

"Bobo, do you *realize* there's a Conway Twitty demon inside your body, trying to make believe he's you?"

But all Bobo said was, "Nobody could do it like Roy Acuff before he got old and started doing sausage commercials."

Of course, we've all heard this before, specially those of

us that work in the evangelism binness, casting out demons on a regular basis. This particular demon was one you don't see much down in Texas, cause it comes from Salina, Kansas, where it lives in a Motel 5. (A Motel 5 is a Motel 6 that'll rent a room to *anybody.*) It's been there since 1963, the only year Conway Twitty ever passed through town, back when people would of paid good money to watch Conway pick his nose. Apparently Conway did pick his nose that night. He picked his nose on stage, bless his heart, and it caused several people to flee from the Kansas Wesleyan College auditorium, creating a temporary vacuum that was filled by a demon that was floating around over by the pizza factory. One way you can always flush this guy out is to say, "Elvis is king," and watch what he does. You got to be careful, cause sometimes he'll start playing Bob Wills songs at 78 rpm and it'll make him sound like an Amana icemaker in there, but usually he'll just flop right out, dead on the ground.

Course, in Bobo's case, this didn't work. I kept yelling "Elvis is king . . . Elvis is king," but the dang thing just kept on uglying around in there, making Bobo's face look like a piece of rotten cabbage, except around the eyes, where it looked like a piece of rotten Velveeta cheese.

"Bobo, I may have to go get Oral Roberts or something," I told him. "I han't been saved long enough to deal with a Conway Twitty demon with no fear of Elvis."

And Bobo said, "Hank Williams died before his time."

And then I knew we had a problem on our hands, so I said, "Bobo, this is it. I didn't wanna have to do this. You know I'm not a violent kind of guy. I hate to use extreme measures. But you know what I have to do?"

"What?"

"I have to beat the shit out of you in a Christian manner."

"Oh."

That's all Bobo said. Just "Oh."

"Bobo?"

He didn't answer me.

"Bobo? You there?"

He went plumb dumb on me. But then I saw his eyes start to move, and I got up real close where I could look at him, and then his mouth opened and his tongue stuck out and wrapped around his neck, and then his eyeballs started spinning around in his sockets, and his ears started flapping like Dumbo the elephant, and the whole right side of his face jumped off and moved over to the left side of his face, and the left side of his face started itching and twitching and finally slid down on his neck, and his neck turned around so his Adam's apple was on the backside, and his haircut started doing the Mexican hat dance, and his hands flew off and landed in the middle of his face, and I started screaming for mercy.

"Bobo, that's disgusting."

But it didn't do any good. And then Bobo's hands started to move, and I said, "No, not *that*. Don't do *that. No, I can't stand it!"*

But it was too late. Bobo was already starting to pick his nose *with both hands.*

I guess it was the first time I ever saw the Conway Twitty demon in person, so I started screaming the lyrics to "Love Me Tender," and when that didn't work I started in on "Jailhouse Rock," and when *that* didn't work, I had to try to remember stuff from *King Creole* like "Hard Headed Woman" and "Dixieland Rock" and the song right after Vic Morrow robs the drugstore where the Big E's dad works and Elvis gets so depressed he falls in love with Dolores Hart. But, I don't know, none of this stuff seemed to work, and meanwhile Bobo's face kept looking more and more like something Pablo Picasso drew up for the wallpaper in his bathroom.

And then, all of a sudden, I screamed, "See you later, Alligator."

Now you're probly wondering why I said that, specially if you're not in the God binness like I am. You see, I had me a Conway Twitty demon and so I *assumed* the only way to fight him was with Elvis lyrics, but what I didn't know was he'd been floating around possessing stupid people like Bobo for about two years by that time and so he was *immune* to Elvis lyrics. He'd heard ever one of em, including "As Long As I Have You," which is exactly what he was singing to Bobo at the time I screamed "See you later, Alligator."

It turns out, if there was one thing the Conway Twitty demon hated more than Elvis, it was Bill Haley and the Comets. Since I could sing the entire soundtrack from *Rock Around the Clock* without even stopping for breath, this demon was a goner. I made him beg for mercy, then I made him put Bobo's face back on right, and then, just to make sure, I took an old dirty tennis shoe and hammered on Bobo's nose a few minutes, and then I made the demon *assure* me that all Bobo's body parts were in their correct positions, and then I stood back from Bobo for a minute and looked at him, and I said, "Bobo, you're still pretty damn ugly."

And Bobo said, "What?"

He was *healed.* It was the old Bobo again. You know, sometimes the Lord works in mysterious ways, and then again sometimes he works in stupid ways.

Anyhow, I got Bobo's head back on straight, but he still didn't get any dates.

One thing I decided after I found out Drive-In Jesus Is Lord is how I had to go out in the desert and be tempted of the devil. Really, I'd just as soon be tempted of the devil in my living room, and I'd specially like to be tempted of

the devil at Geno's Topless on Harry Hines Boulevard in
Dallas, but meantime we were fresh out of Vision Beer
and so I said goodbye to Bobo and told him I was heading
down to the Chihuahuan Desert to be tempted of the
devil.

Bobo said, "Humpa-humpa?"

And I said, "No, Bobo, West Texas. Not Mexico. I'm goin
to West Texas."

And Bobo went back to combing his face.

To tell you the truth, I was starting to get a little worried
about the strength of my faith. After the night when I got
saved, I got kicked out of ever decent drive-in between
Amarillo and El Paso, and all the indecent ones except for
the Twin Three's Drive-In in Canyon, and they only let
me in there cause I told em I was a relative of Jumbalaya
Briggs, the famous Cajun Indian fighter that killed nineteen Blackfoot Indians for pourin Heinz ketchup on fried
eggs.

And *why*? Why do you think I was persecuted
everwhere I went?

Cause they didn't believe me. They thought I was a liar.
They called me a deadbeat, a loafer, an unemployed
drifter. You couldn't *believe* the persecution from some of
these people. They said I stole stuff. They said I operated
illegal gambling operations. They claimed I was wanted
for grand-theft auto in three states.

But you see what I'm talking about here? You *see* the
kind of distortions and lies I had to deal with on a daily
basis? So I packed it in, fired up the Bel Air, and headed
south to find spiritual knowledge and a little free nookie.

Bobo took it pretty hard. On the day I left, he followed
me out to the Frontage Road city limits, where they have
the government dirt office, and he said, "What if head go
crooked again?"

And I saw a tear start to form in Bobo's left eyeball, and for a minute I thought I was gonna get all choked up myself, and then I just said, "Hell, Bobo, you don't even *need* a head."

That seemed to cheer him up a little bit. So I said, "If I ever meet Oral Roberts, I'll ask him to make you up a new one."

But all Bobo could manage was one little puny "Humpa." I couldn't hardly stand it to watch a Pawnee with thighs like Bobo's starting to cry, so I turned on my heel and walked away. Actually, first I fell down from trying to turn around on my heel, but then I walked away and fired up the Merc and I looked out the window, and there was Bobo, standing by the Pawnee Wagon, staring at his Hush Puppies and running his hands all over his face to make sure it was still there.

"Bobo," I yelled at him, "someday I'll come back as a famous religious preacher who can get people to give him money just for struttin around the high school coliseum."

But Bobo wasn't listening. Bobo was putting on his feather bonnet so he could get a ride back in to Frontage Road by impersonating an Apache Medicine Man.

I couldn't take the sight of it. I stomped on the brake and fishtailed across the highway and spun around so I was facing Bobo.

"Bobo," I said, "get in."

Bobo didn't hear me cause he was already blowin peace-pipe smoke rings through his nose.

"Bobo!" I screamed at him. He looked up, with his usual blank expression. I nodded for him to get in.

Bobo just stood there.

"Get in," I said.

Bobo got an expression on his face like he forgot where the toilet paper was.

"Humpa-humpa," I told him.

Bobo took off runnin, jumped into the passenger seat, and rearranged his body hair to keep peelings from off my upholstery. He was one happy Pawnee.

7

How I Invented the Titty Bar

Me and Bobo hit the road.

Now that I think about it, lookin back on the day I tore down Texas Route 214 trying to find a public restroom, that was when the magic started. That's the day I started out on the Joe Bob Briggs Road to Spiritual Success. Course, I didn't know it at the time. All God said to me on the way out of town was, "Joe Bob, ye have been separated out from mankind. Go ye and seek out the rich people and ye beautiful women and make them do whatever ye want them to." Course, this is the essence of evangelism. It's a lonely job, but I was prepared to sacrifice my body and my soul for all the people who deserved me.

But there was something I had to do first. Before I could start telling people how they were going to Hell, I had to go out in the desert and be tempted of the Devil. So I started out for Mescalero, New Mexico, cause that's where the Apache savages worship the ancient peyote plant and if I was gonna be tempted, I wanted to go with the hard stuff. But I only got as far as Hobbs before I started to fag out, and so I stopped in at Furr's Cafeteria to chew some beef and preach some drive-in gospel, and while I was in there I met this guy named Walter Walter. His first name was Walter and his last name was Walter, and he had a little brother named Walter and a son on the way named Walter Walter, Jr., and his great grandfather was also named Walter Walter, after the Walter Walter who fought in the War to Carve Up Europe into Itty Bitty Pieces. It wasn't a very famous war, but I just mention it cause of the name Walter Walter, in case you heard it before.

Walter Walter has nothin to do with this book, so I'm kickin him out of it right now.

But the reason I bring it up is cause it was Walter Walter that first told me how to get out of Hobbs, New Mexico, and get started on my life. I'll never forget what he said to me that day. He said, "Joe Bob, I love you."

Walter Walter was a disgusting drunk of the homosexual persuasion.

So Bobo and me decided to skip the dessert part and go straight for the groceries. Bobo picked up Walter Walter by the nape of the neck and said, "Hasta la cabeza," which is basically Bobo's way of saying "I'm about to dribble your head on the concrete." And so I told Bobo it was time to get back on the road of life, and suddenly Walter Walter's eyes rolled up in the back of his head and he looked at me and he said, "The road of life is U.S. 180 East."

As I said, sometimes the Lord works in stupid ways.

And I said, "I just come in on 180."

And he said, "Well, maybe it's 176 East, but in that case you need to haul your ass down to Eunice, New Mexico, and hit the cutoff, or else you could go over to Carlsbad and try 285, but that's going a long way out of the way and you might end up in Pecos and there's no place to eat there."

And then after Bobo finished beatin him up, we started our destinies.

You're probly wondering why I took U.S. 180 East to start out my life. Don't wonder about it anymore, though, cause I didn't. I moseyed over to Carlsbad and took 285 south back into Texas, cause one thing I just *hate* is doubling back into counties where they got my name. But it *is* pretty funny that most books about civilization start out in the East and they go West, but this one starts out in the West and goes East, except for the part right here where I'm going South so I can get back on a decent highway.

I was sick and tired of the wilderness. God didn't tempt me with anything worth a damn out there, and so I was ready to go tempt my ownself a little bit. I talked to God about it and decided what I needed was a mate. Bobo nodded stupidly, climbed into the backseat while the car was moving, flopped on the cushion, and imitated a beached alligator gar dying very slowly.

Alone with my thoughts, I started gettin real excited about havin a real woman that wasn't Beanstalk Jailbait, Thunder Thighs, or a Lipstick Lizard, although a Lipstick Lizard would be okay just to start off.

I really wasn't too particular about it. I'd accept *any* mate God sent me, only I told God a few things to put on her so I'd recognize true love when it come along.

I knew she'd be the kind of woman that had inner beauty. She'd have so much inner beauty that you'd be able to see it on the outer.

She'd be full of virtue. She wouldn't go to bed with me on the first date, unless I got her drunk and slapped her around a little bit.

She'd love long walks in the park, and she'd find some idiot to go do that with her.

Other than those things, I wouldn't care—any bimbo God wanted to send me, it didn't make a flip to me. And also she had to have hooters the size of Wisconsin.

Bobo said his had to have teeth. Bobo remembered that time in the border town.

So I tooled down 285, looking for hitchhiking sluts, figuring God would put one on the side of the road for me, but all I found was this skinny little hippie goat-roper with some peach fuzz on his chin and a jacket that said "ARISE!" on the back shoulder and he was carrying a two-ply No. 10 Safeway grocery bag under one arm and a can of Beanee Weenees under the other arm and he was thumbing a ride when I went by him. And so I pulled over and stopped and looked back at him, and I rolled down my window and yelled, "Is all you got to eat a can of Beanee Weenees?"

And he just kind of nodded his head. And I said, "Can I have some of em?"

And that's how I met Rhett Beavers. Years later I'd replay this incident over and over in my mind, and I'd say, "Rhett, why were you carrying the Beanee Weenees like that when you had a Safeway bag?"

And Rhett would say, "They're better than Spam."

That's how I knew Rhett was my kind of guy. He talked in philosophy all the time, cause he'd been out to Mescalero to see the snake doctors and eat dirt-on-a-biscuit and do whatever else they do to scare the prairie dogs, and so anytime I had a question I could just ask Rhett.

"Where you goin with that haircut?" was the first thing I asked him when he got in the car. Rhett's hair looked like he was doing zebra autopsies up there.

"Sonora. Goat Capital of the World."

"You kiddin me?"

"Sure," he said. "All that desert's good for is raising Mohair sweaters."

"What you lookin for in Sonora?"

"Goat knowledge."

"That's a coincidence. I'm lookin for God to send me a wife."

Rhett looked pleased.

"Did He say He would?"

"Before I answer that," I told him, "I need to know if you been saved or not."

"They said I was saved in Ko Rea, but I don't know if it counts."

"Yeah, it probly counts. Were you saved by a white man?"

"He said he was."

"It counts."

"So," Rhett said, "if I been saved, then what did God say?"

"He didn't say jack. I told Him what I wanted, told Him to put hooters on her so I'd see her comin, and you're the only thing I picked up for two hunnerd miles now."

"Where'd you get them cutaway speakers?"

"Northside a Lubbock."

Rhett and me could talk all day like this, discussing the meaning of life. We never did say "Hi hire yew" or nothin, we just started in talkin and we been talkin ever since. We talked all the way through Pecos and Fort Stockton and down to Langtry and Del Rio, and then Rhett got a little nervous and lit up some Polio Weed and I couldn't help noticing when his face started resembling a piece of baloney that's been sittin on top of the refrigerator for six weeks and so I said, "Beavers, you get that stuff from one of them Apache witch doctors?"

And Rhett said, "Grow it in my backyard."

"You know you can get freeze-dried for doing that? It's American law that you can only do that in Mexico."

"My backyard's in Mexico."

"Oh."

Rhett always abided by the law, even when he got arrested.

"Rhett, what you think about this wife deal?"

"You wanna marry somebody?"

"No, I just want a wife."

"Good idea."

"You know any?"

"I know one wife," Rhett said, "but she's married."

"All the wives I ever heard of are married."

"I could use one myself."

"Really? You don't look like it."

"That's what the wives say."

I considered that a minute, and then I said, "We may have to find us some unmarried ones."

"Would they still be wives?"

"Not unless we really screwed up."

"That's a great idea."

And so that's when Rhett and me and Bobo decided to go lookin for nookie together. Actually Bobo didn't decide, cause Bobo was in the backseat makin a sound like a buffalo gettin his appendix took out, but we counted Bobo in because Bobo's entire life had been devoted to the gathering of nookie.

There was only one problem. We're talkin early sixties, and there was so much makeup out there on the market that you couldn't hardly examine the merchandise without spraying Lysol on ever bimbo you met and then scrubbing em clean to the bone. Like one time I met this girl named Phoebe Box, and she had long blonde hair like Lassie and a face that could of directed the Mormon Tabernacle Choir and a chest that looked like she spent all morning setting up two Army tents in there.

You should of seen her the next morning. She was in so many pieces we had to go out and buy an Erector set to figure out how to put her back together again. Her blonde hair was evidently built in one of the oil refineries down on the coast, cause when she tossed it under the bed all the roaches died of fumes. By the time she finished washing her face, we had to have the entire geology department at Texas A&M come out and identify the rock formations in the sink. And the worst part of it was, she *did* have two Army tents set up in there.

All I got to say is, I wish I could make like Ray Milland in *X: The Man With the X-Ray Eyes,* when he throws some chemicals on his face and then goes to all these wild parties and stares through the bimbos' dresses while they're doing the Frug, cause it makes you disgusted right away and you don't have to waste a bunch of gas money on spoiled meat. What I'm trying to say is, there ain't no good way to do it.

But then I got this idea. Actually, me and Rhett got this same idea at the same time, cause we were driving up towards Sonora and starting to see some Angora goats out there on the rocks, dreaming that someday they'd be rubbing up against Jayne Mansfield's Playtex triple-Ds, and all of a sudden I remembered this scene in *Bell, Bare and Beautiful* where Virginia Bell puts these little whirlybirds on her garbonzas and starts making a hurricane.

"Yeah, I remember it," Rhett said.

"One thing about Virginia Bell, she had the biggest boobs in the greater Cincinnati area and everbody knew it."

"Yeah."

"And the *reason* everbody knew it is she could flop em on cue."

"Yeah."

"They were more than just boobies."

"Lots more."

"They were *performers.*"

Rhett didn't say nothing.

"Virginia Bell had so much talent up there she needed three agents."

"I could of handled her," Rhett said.

"Are you an agent, too?"

"No, but I could of handled her."

"That's just it, we *all* could of handled her."

"She oughta donate those things to the Smithsonian Museum."

"I don't think they allow female jugs in the Smithsonian Museum."

"I believe they'd make an exception," Rhett said. "You couldn't call em jugs, though."

"No."

"Have to call em succulent mounds."

"Yeah. You know, another thing about Virginia Bell. She could make those Mount Nebos do more tricks than Rin Tin Tin."

"That's a fact," he said. "Or they could call em Human Himalayas."

"Shoot, they need a pole vaulter just to see the top of em."

"Maybe they could call em Titanic Titties."

Anyhow, we went on like this for a while, discussing the eighth and ninth wonders of the western world, when I said, "Heck, *that's it. I wanna get married to Virginia Bell!*"

And Rhett said, "How about Hippo Hooters?"

"Listen to me, Beavers, I wanna marry em . . . I wanna marry her!"

"No way, José. She's in the movies. She can have any guy in Cincinnati she wants."

And I said, "But I'm in love with her."

And Rhett said, "What do you think of Great Big Old Bazoomas?"

"I'm in love with her."

"Shoot, we can find better titties than that."

"There ain't no better titties."

"I hear they got some in Houston so big they gotta close off a lane of traffic ever time she gets in her car."

"Yeah, I heard about em, too, but she's one of them *married* wives."

"There's probly titties like that hidin under goat sweaters all over Texas."

"I guess if they had some out here, you wouldn't know it, cause there's not enough traffic."

"How about just Double Hulk?"

Sometimes me and Rhett thought on the same wavelength.

We were ridin by one of Ozona's finer restaurants, called "B-B-Q," and I said, "You know, there could be titties in that place there, just crying to get out."

Rhett looked over at B-B-Q and said, "Nope. Too little. Couldn't get Virginia Bell's titties through that door."

"I guess you're right."

Then we didn't say anything for a while, but when we got to the other end of town we saw another restaurant, called "EAT."

By that time I'd already finished off all Rhett's Beanee Weenees, so I said, "You hungry?"

"I could do with some goat meat," Rhett said.

And so I pulled in at EAT, which had a big wide door on it, and we went inside and got a booth and stared at the waitress's chest when she came up to the table, and after about two minutes it started to bother her and she said, "Do you know what you want?"

And Rhett said, "Yes, Ma'am, two please."

And she said, "Two what?"

And I said, "Do you ever have any trouble pulling out on the highway?"

And she said, "Sometimes."

And I said, "What's your name?"

"Vida Stegall."

"Vida, may I call you Vida?"

"Of course."

"Vida, I'll have two over easy."

"And what about him?"

"Vida, he's speechless."

"Okay, I'll come back later."

"Vida?"

"Yes?"

"Show me your tits."

After we got out of the Ozona Jail, Rhett had this great binness idea. He couldn't stop talking about it. He kept saying that we were in the heart of Bazooma Country and why not take advantage of it?

"I never knew why they called this the Hill Country," he said to me.

"But it's no good, Rhett," I kept telling him. "They don't wanna show em down here. It ain't like Cincinnati."

But Rhett said, "We'll put on titty fashion shows, and the whole *city* will come out to look at em."

"Rhett, there ain't such a thing as titty fashion shows."

"Why not?"

"Cause there ain't such a thing as titty fashions."

"What about Virginia Bell's whirlybirds?"

"It's only people up north that buy that stuff."

"Okay, so we put on titty fashion shows and all the people up north come down here to look at em."

Obviously, Rhett finally said something that made sense, so I said I'd give it a try. And I won't go through all the high-level discussions that led up to it, but that's basically how the first titty bar in America was born. There was a lot of people that tried to *act* like they started titty bars: burlesque shows, go-go clubs, those places in Cuba where they teach titties to do the rumba. But the first *real* titty bar was on Highway 290 between Ozona and Sonora, out there where you can still tell the difference between the goats and most of the women.

I know. We owned it.

The idea was gonna be that I was the talent manager and musical director, and Rhett was the binness manager, and Bobo was the bouncer and master of ceremonies. And if we discovered any legitimate wife material in the daily cattle call, I got to marry her for at least one day. What we did is, we rented a big old cinder-block shearing shed set back off the highway, and then we started putting in some lava lamps and strobe lights and a great Sears sound system, and when it was about ready to open, we put this ad in ever newspaper between San Angelo and Laredo. Here's what it said:

Wanted: Girls with enormous talents, for special medical experiment. Please send photo, color if possible, of largest gland on upper torso. Take photo in extremely cold room for maximum exposure. Send to Dr. Joseph Robert Briggs, c/o "Chez Highway 290," Rural Route 3, Sonora, Tex. Please enclose marital status and whether you're a slut or not. Thank you.

I made a big mistake by using a medical word like "Gland" in the ad, cause we got some *disgusting* stuff in the mailbox. It got so bad the mailman said he wasn't delivering to us no more unless the USDA checked his pouch for bacteria ever morning. But, of course, we got flooded with applications from all over the greater Sonora area. We had to narrow em down one by one, call em in to talk things over, interview em, audition em, see how they could dance, find out if they could talk English—we pretty much had to put em through the old meat grinder. Pretty soon we were gonna have some of the most amazing boobs in West Texas waltzing across the shearing shed.

Actually, we only got one application, but there's a perfectly good explanation for that.

A lot of the girls read the ad *and they didn't know it was a titty bar.* Course, how could you be expected to know in those days? You walk up to somebody in 1963 and you say,

"I own a titty bar," and they think you're crazy. I had to educate the entire nation before we'd get the titty-bar idea started.

Anyhow, this one ole gal comes by, named Joyce Karnes. And I wouldn't say Joyce had the most gigantic B-52s in the whole known universe, but she had more up front than Rhett and me and so I auditioned her to the Meat Market theme song, *Climb Ever Mountain*, and she could pretty much stay on the beat as long as you didn't confuse her by talkin or moving your body while she was up there. We planned it so at the end of the song, she was gonna whip off her Dacron Annette Funicello tube-top foam-rubber-support turquoise swimming vest right at the moment when Jim Nabors hit the high note, and then she was gonna make those boobs finish the song.

The only problem is, you don't know what boobs'll do until you get em in front of a live audience. And the funny thing is, it had nothing to do with size. You can get little ones that do thirty Broadway show tunes in a row, and you can get humongous ones that freeze up onstage and just lay there like a couple of watery sno-cones. It's tough when something like that happens, cause it's hard to keep your dignity.

On opening night we were ready for anything. Joyce was a little nervous so I took her backstage for some psychological counseling.

"Now Joyce," I told her, "I hope you realize we're making American history tonight, and it's all resting on your chest."

She nodded demurely and then spelled it.

"You're not just doing this for yourself, you know. You're three people tonight."

She counted herself slowly.

"And I don't wanna see you doing anything lewd or disgusting on the stage that would embarrass your country. We're gonna have a shed full of horny cowboys out there, and they'd be mighty disappointed if you did anything that the County Sheriff would be ashamed of."

"Mr. Briggs?"

"Yes?"

"Can I get nekkid now?"

That's the kind of girl Joyce was, always ready to exhibit the groceries.

"Of course you can, dear. Here, gimme two kisses."

"Joe Bob?"

"Yes."

"Can I do my medley from *Oklahoma*?"

"Now Joyce, you remember what I said about being lewd or disgusting on the stage?"

"Can I just sing 'I'm Gonna Wash that Man Right Out of My Hair'?"

"Joyce, we're gonna have members of the Texas State legislature out there tonight."

"Well, can I just put my fists on my hips and belt one out, like 'No Binness Like Show Binness,' or maybe 'Everthang's Comin Up Roses'?"

"Joyce, I'll let you do all the show tunes on Tuesday nights from 4 to 6, but right now I just want you to concentrate on the number we already worked on."

"Which one?"

" 'I Only Have Thighs for You.' "

"Okay. Joe Bob, I won't let you down. I'll sing my little heart out."

"Joyce, you still don't understand. *No singing.* I'll put the record on, you come out and do the rumba and move your lips like you're singin, and then at the very end, when we get to the last chorus, on the word 'thighs,' I want you to spring em out of the chute."

"Nipples first?"

"No, I want whirlybirds on em."

"Whirlybirds?"

And then it hit me. "Heck, *I forgot to buy whirlybirds!* Durn! Rhett was supposed to remind me and . . . wait a minute . . . I got an idea . . . Here, use these. The crowd'll never know the difference."

"You want me to put these on my breasts?"

"Only on the front of em."

"What if they go off?"

"They won't go off as long as you don't light em up."

"No! It's too dangerous. I could poke a breast out with one of them things."

"Just get some Elmer's and stick em on there like *this,* and like *this,* and like *this,* and like *this,* with the exploding part stuck directly on the fleshy part of the titty proper."

"No! Absolutely no!"

"Joyce, you do this to me now and I'm finished. It's either this or we paint Captain Kangaroo characters on your tits so we can tell the cops it's a kiddie show."

"You wouldn't!"

"Joyce, trust me. Put these on your tits, be a trouper, and I'll let you sing 'Some Enchanted Evening' next week."

"What about my dramatic reading with harp accompaniment?"

"Joyce, this is not the Miss Texas Pageant, what you think we got here, perverts?"

I kind of hurt Joyce's feelings when I said that, cause she gets upset when I yell at her, and so I said, "Look, I'm sorry. We can talk later. But right now you need to stick these sizzlers on your headlamps so we can start the show. We got three hunnerd raving citizens out there, it's the Fourth of July, and Rhett just had to send over to Sonora for some more goat nachos. *Please.* You got nothin to

worry about. Just keep jiggling and they won't care. Let
your Almond Joys do all the work."

"Joe Bob, I'm scared."

"I know you are, honey, but remember, it's not you out
there, it's your Mama Leones."

"You're right."

"Okay, let's go over the rules one more time. Rule number one."

"Always bounce vertically, never sideways."

"Very good. Rule numero two-o."

"Always remember where I am on the stage."

"Why?"

She thought for a minute. "So I don't damage the customers with my tits?"

"No, so you don't get sweat in the drinks."

"Oh yeah."

"Okay, and rule numero three-o?"

"Use ever inch. Never give em the whole potato all at
once."

"You got it. And, by the way, Joyce . . ."

"Yes."

"You got Idaho grade A's."

She blushed. "I just hope they don't freeze up on me."

"Don't say that. Now knock em dead."

"I thought you didn't want me to . . ."

"No, you're right, don't knock em dead. Just keep em
under control and do the encores one tit at a time."

"I love you, Joe Bob."

That's the kind of bullstuff I was afraid of, cause, frankly,
Joyce was uglier than a bullfrog with acne, but I didn't let
on, cause when you're in the titty binness, you take the
titties anywhere you can find em.

You should of seen the place that night: July 4, 1964. We
had a big sign outside— "CHEZ HIGHWAY 290"—and
underneath that we wrote in "A Club for Gentlemen and

Their Sleazy Friends." One time we got wrote up in *Cava-lier* magazine, and here's what they said about us:

"Readers in Texas report a night-club, hidden away on an isolated goat ranch, where bestiality is openly practiced."

When that come out, I showed it to Honey Heather, our best dancer, and she said, "What's bestiality?"

And I said, "That's *you*. They're saying how you're openly practiced."

"Does that mean I practice a lot?"

"Yeah, and it's the opposite of worstiality."

So after that we changed the sign out front and wrote on it "Ask Us About Our Bestiality," and binness picked up quite a bit from then on. But that was a couple years later, after we were famous. Back on the Fourth of July opening night, things were a little shaky.

Joyce did fine at first. She come out shakin and bakin like a plate of strawberry Jell-O, but the animals in the audience just stared at her all during the "Theme From Beach Party" number. I remember she had enough mascara and gook around her eyes to audition for Barnum and Bailey, but nobody was lookin at her eyes. They were staring at the big white bow on the front of her prom dress, cause they knew at some point she was gonna pull on that sucker and spring her Pop-Tarts. So then she moved into "Let's Do the Twist," the original Chubby version, and that heated em up a little bit cause under her dress she didn't have a brassiere and she was obviously hiding a few of the neighboring counties on her chest. And finally, we got to the payoff number, "I Only Have Thighs for You," and by then the audience was getting a little unruly, specially Lester Scranton, who drove down all the way from Austin and was investigating us for the Texas Rangers. Lester said if he didn't see some decent boobies, he was gonna arrest us for public lewdness on a goat ranch.

Actually, I was countin *very* heavily on gettin arrested that night. I had my overnight bag packed, I had a statement about Communist censorship ready to read to the reporters, and I had some spare handcuffs under the bar in case Lester tried to arrest me without cuffs.

"Rhett," I said that afternoon, "I don't want nobody arrested without cuffs, cause it looks better in the newspapers. Specially Joyce. If they don't cuff her, then I want *you* to cuff her from behind."

"I don't know, Joe Bob, I think you can get in trouble for going around putting handcuffs on people."

"Only if they don't like it. Joyce *loves* handcuffs."

"Oh."

So anyhow, I had the cuffs ready, and I had Lester in the audience (I greeted Lester personally at the door and said, "Lester, I want you to know we got some nasty illegal stuff goin on in here tonight"), and I had Joyce's Grand Tetons open for tourism.

Like I say, everthing started out okay, and we got clean through to the "Thighs" number with Joyce doin the rumba, the twist, and a modern-jazz interpretive dance. The reason I know it was a modern-jazz interpretive dance is she told me afterwards, right after I screamed at her, "What the flying Frito was *that?*" And she said it was a modern-jazz interpretive dance. It's basically where somebody puts on a fart record and Joyce imitates a horny kangaroo. I told her to never let it happen again. It was a good thing everbody was drunk as the U.S. Congress, cause otherwise they would of noticed Joyce could dance about as good as the muscular-dystrophy poster child.

Finally, though, we got clean through to the moment of truth. I was running the record player, and I had Perry Como's version of "I Only Have Thighs for You," with

Rhett shoutin out "Thighs!" ever time the word came up, only he generally shouted it out about three beats too late, but anyhow I was startin to feel good about the whole thing. The crowd was getting rowdy, but we'd only had three, four people carried out on stretchers, which is pretty good for that part of West Texas, and you could tell they knew it was comin. One way you could tell it was comin is Joyce kept testing her bow to see if she knew how to get the sucker untied. But the goat-ropers knew something humongous was about to spill out of the Hoover Dam, and they started tiltin back in their chairs and puttin their cigarettes out and wipin their sleeves across their mouths like gentlemen.

And finally Rhett yelled out the last *"Thighs!"* just as loud as he could do it, and Joyce stopped dancin, put both hands on her bow, and ripped her blouse clean off her body. There was an agonizing second of suspense that seemed like hundreds of thousands of years as her titties hung suspended in the air, and then went *thwack*.

That's the noise they made when they flopped out: *thwack*.

The reason I know that's the noise they made is it was the only noise in the club.

The place went dead. Joyce stood there with her jugs hanging loose, and everbody just stared at em. No clappin, no yee-hawin, no nothin. I wasn't sure what was goin on, so finally I yelled out, "How about another big Thwack for the boys here, Joyce." And so Joyce jumped up on her high heels and flopped em again.

The second time she did it, Lester Scranton turned around and looked at me and said, "Hell, Briggs, I oughta arrest you for false advertising."

And I said, "Hell, Lester, they're not atomic missiles, but they're 32s."

"They might be 32s if you inflated em to about double size."

And I looked at em and Lester was right. Joyce had Silly Putty for boobs, and at the moment they were laying down like salami slices on vacation.

"Thwack em again, Joyce!" I screamed.

And then all hell broke loose. "Please no, don't do it," somebody yelled, and then they all started screamin to *please, don't do that thwack thing again.* It was sort of like the sound of fingernails on a chalkboard, it was just somethin you can't listen to without gettin sick at your stomach.

People started gettin up to leave, and so I jumped up onstage and begged em to stay.

"Really, she can do more than thwack em," I said. "She can make these titties do anything you want."

"Can she inflate em?" some guy yelled.

And then I saw Lester hisself gettin up to leave, and I said, "Lester, you han't even arrested anybody yet."

And Lester said, "I'm about ready to arrest those titties for loitering!"

You know, some people can be cruel.

I jumped down off the stage, screaming at everbody to stay, and I saw my life pass before my eyes. I realized for the first time that my entire future life depended on two boobs that I didn't even know that well, and it all seemed so unfair, and I didn't know how I was gonna save myself, when suddenly I heard a loud hissing sound behind me, like a rattler that's about to pounce, and I looked around, and there was Joyce, *lighting up her tits.*

I forgot about the firecrackers. We had tied six firecrackers to her boobs to cover up the nipples, and now she was putting a match up to her chest in an attempt to commit breast-a-cide.

"Joyce, don't do it! It's not worth it!"

She didn't seem to hear me. She put the match up to the other boob.

"Joyce, the furniture's rented!"

But it was too late. There was nothing I could say. It took about five seconds for the fuses to burn down, and then they all went off at once. I heard the explosion, but I couldn't stand to look. I dived under a table and started to cry. I prayed she wouldn't burn the place down.

It seemed like an eternity—the explosion was a chain reaction that seemed to last an hour—and then all I heard was screams and shrieks and the pounding of boots on the floor and Rhett standing on the bar and screaming, "She did it! She really did it!"

And all I could think of was I was gonna get hauled in for accessory-to-murder now. I crawled up from under the table, still afraid to look at the stage.

Then I saw the look in Lester Scranton's eyes, and I knew something was terrible terrible wrong. Lester's eyes were spread open wider than I've ever seen em in my life, and he had one of those I-just-got-Ernest-Tubb's-autograph grins on his face, and he couldn't take his eyes off *whatever it was* on the stage.

I was still too scared to turn around myself, but then everbody in the place started shouting "More! Encore! Hoist Them Hooters!" and all the other traditional stuff you yell at a night-club. And so I finally looked around, and there was Joyce, standing straight up in the middle of the stage, nothin left on her boobs but huge black circles around the nipples, and they were floppin around like they had Meskin jumping beans inside em. I swear they kept hoppin and rollin around for two, three minutes after I first turned around, and all Joyce did was stand there beaming like she just got crowned Miss Goat Industry.

I wanted to marry her right then and there. It was the first time in my life a girl ever set her tits on fire for me.

Later on I got the whole story. Joyce was so disappointed when her tits didn't flop on cue—it was partly my fault, cause I told her about how Virginia Bell could *always* flop on cue—that she didn't even think about the personal danger. She grabbed this old boy's matches that was sitting on the front row and went to work. Once she got em lit, she heaved out her chest, and the impact of the explosion caused her to do a double back flip, and then the momentum of her tits continuing to do the rumba spun her around three, four times while the smoke cleared, and then the applause started her adrenaline pumping and so she squeezed em a few times and they started singing "The Star-Spangled Banner" and doing production numbers from *West Side Story.* All I caught was the tail end of the routine, when her titties were all tuckered out.

Course, the legend of what happened that night probly got a few silicone injections over the years, but I basically believe it except for the part about her spinning around. I think she only spun around once or twice, cause I know how easy it is for Joyce to get dizzy.

Like I say, I decided to marry her that very night, even though she only had hooters the size of Delaware.

"Joyce," I said, "I want you to be my wife."

She said, "Huh?"

I said, "By the way, where you from?"

And she went into this long story about how she was from Abilene and her granddaddy was a buffalo hunter and she left home when she was fourteen so she wouldn't have to play the violin anymore, and I said, "Okay, good enough for me."

And she said, "What?"

Joyce and Bobo had a lot in common.

8

El Wedding

We were married that night in Ciudad Acuna, which is Meskin for "Coon City." We had to get the Alcalde out of bed to marry us. He was pretty p.o.ed when we did it, cause the Alcalde is not the guy who's supposed to marry you. So we said we were sorry and gave him some "el money," and then we went all over town looking for somebody that could marry us. Fortunately I speak a little Spanish, so I could walk up to people on the street and say "We-o need el marry-o" and they always knew exactly what I meant. So I guess we did this two, three hours, and we finally found this guy named Poncho or something who said, "I'll marry you for fifty pesos." When I heard him use the word "pesos," I knew we had us a real Spanish-speaking "el padre," and so I gave him five bucks and he married us right away and sold us a solid gold wedding ring for 40 cents, and then he said, "Why you want to be married in Mehico?"

And I said, "Cause we wanted to do it in a hurry."

And he said, "It only takes five minutes on the American side."

Of course, I *knew* that all the time, but I thought it would be romantic to walk all over Coon City for four hours, spreading my money among the Meskin people.

After we were married, we decided to call each other

by our Meskin names from then on. She called me "José."
And I called her "José."

We didn't have much of a honeymoon. We spent it in
the backseat of the Mercury, cause I blew the whole gate
from Chez Highway 290 on "la beera." Actually, *she*
spent it in the backseat of the Mercury, and I spent it on
the floor, passed out from "la beera too mucha."

The next night we went right back to work, cause now
we were the hottest thing in goat country. My wife was
now billed as "The Exploding Tit Woman." We worked it
into the act, and for the next two years, she blew her tits
up, twice a night like clockwork. Some women wouldn't
have understood a husband that made em do that. They
would have thought it was "kinky" or "dirty" or "dangerous."

But not José.

I loved her like a trained pet. There wasn't anything I
wouldn't do for José, except maybe co-sign on a car note.
A few months after the club opened, Rhett tried to add a
new number to her routine. He wanted her to balance a
glass of water on her left tit while she was doing ventrilo-
quism. It was something Rhett saw her do at a party.

But I said, "No way, José."

My wife still had her dignity.

Of course, we had a lot of other girls come through the
Chez Highway 290. We had girls that worked with boa
constrictors, girls that could strip nekkid while standing
on their hands, we even had one girl that could dance. But
none of em were like José. She was the first and she was
the best. You know, in future years many professional
bimbos would come along, *trying* to explode their tits, but
just think about it. Did you ever see *one* that could do the
double backflip without cheating? It was a natural God-
given talent.

Long as we had José, we didn't have to worry about

much of anything else. After a while, Rhett hired him a bartender and went back to Mexico to tend Polio Weed. We'd see him once or twice a month, when he'd come north to see all his close personal friends and exchange pleasantries, if you know what I mean and I think you do. I convinced Lester to arrest me a couple times, but he wanted so much money for it, it wasn't hardly worth it after a while. Bobo became the "Voice of Chez Highway 290," cause he never did say anything, which was how the customers liked it, and ever few days I'd make Bobo happy by lettin him stick one of the non-paying customers on a giant cactus and play "Pin the Rattlesnake on the Human." It was one of Bobo's favorite games. And ever Monday morning we'd audition titties.

Titties descended on Highway 290 from all over the greater Southwest. One time we had a set of tits drive in all the way from Durant, Oklahoma, just to see if they had the "stuff." A lot of times I'd have to be honest with these girls.

I'd say, "Look, you and fifty million other girls in America wanna work here, but it's not all glamor. It's a lot of hard work, too. Have you ever looked at some of the older girls, really *studied* the shape of their tits. *Years* of training to get that. You can't just waltz in here in a cashmere sweater and expect me to put you up there next to professional trained garbonzas. A lot of these tits have agents. Most of em have two agents."

But, you know, they don't listen. Then, when we'd take the 1 or 2 per cent that *did* have trainable titties, a lot of times we'd have to trick em up, give em the Maybelline treatment, use special effects and gadgets. One gal, we had to train two weenie-dogs to sit up on top of her titties, just so people'd have something to look at.

"You know, Rhett," I said one afternoon, "titties aren't all they're cut out to be."

"What you mean?"

"You ever really take a good hard look at em?"

"Can't say that I have."

"Couple a tetherballs hanging off your chest. Now you call that sexy?"

"Can't say that I do, no."

"Couple a tetherballs, just hanging there, waiting to be squeezed."

"Pretty disgusting."

"Course, some of em aren't even tetherballs."

"Nope."

"Bean bags."

"You said it."

"Bean bags is all they are. Or mothballs."

"Mothballs. Those are the worst ones."

"So what's the big deal about tits?"

"I don't know."

"We *oughta* know. We're in that binness. It's our binness to know. But we don't know."

"That's right. We don't know."

"Most binnesses, they don't have to worry about tits."

"No."

"Oil binness. Tits don't matter."

"Nope."

"Hardware store. You don't even *need* tits for a hardware store."

"I never thought of it."

"But we gotta think about *tits* all the time."

"It's a bummer."

"Sometimes I feel like tellin em to keep their tops on."

"I know what you mean."

"I mean all the time. I mean *never* show their tits."

"Might help."

"Shoot, binness would probly go *up.*"

"Probly."

"People are sick and tired of tits around here."

"May be."

"You ever seen a bimbo that *didn't* have tits?"

"Once or twice."

"Maybe we need one of them."

"Uh-huh."

"Might liven things up around here."

"We could use *that.*"

"Course, then it wouldn't be a titty bar, would it?"

"I guess not."

"Not a very good idea, is it?"

"Probly need another one."

"God, I hate tits."

"Even José's tits?"

"Well, I guess a man is obliged to love his wife's tits, but sometimes even hers get on my nerves."

"Do José's tits ever get mushy from being blowed up all the time?"

"Rhett, I can't believe you'd ask me a question like that. What do you think José is, a piece of meat?"

"I'm sorry, I wasn't thinking."

"It's okay. Go set up the titty trapeze."

"Right."

This next part of the story is tough for me to admit. I don't know how it happened. I don't know why it happened. I don't know who it happened with. I don't know who I should of murdered when it did happen. I don't know where it happened or which direction it happened. I only know it happened.

One day I woke up and José was gone.

She didn't say nothing. The night before she blew up her tits at 8, 10, and midnight, as usual. We went to bed about 2. I woke up at 10 and she'd cleaned out the regular closet *and* the bra closet and left. All I found was a note on the dresser.

"Dear José," it said, "I owe you a lot. You made me what I am today. I couldn't have done it without you. I don't expect you to understand what's happening right now, but I've got to leave. The reason may not seem very important to you, but years from now you'll understand: my titties hurt. Love, José."

That's all it said. No explanation. No way for me to reach her. I ran down to the Greyhound station, hoping I could catch her or find somebody that knew where she was going, but there was no sign of her anywhere. I went back to the club and put a sign up: "No Exploding Tits Tonight." But I was so depressed that, after a while, I went back outside and scratched out "Exploding." It was the first time in two years the club was closed.

"How could she do it?" I asked Rhett later. "How could she leave this life and go back to whatever she was in civilian clothes?"

"Hard to figure out," Rhett said, "unless . . ."

"Unless what?"

"Unless one of the big mass-market titty-bar chains up north offered her a contract."

"But Rhett, she was my *wife.*".

"Joe Bob, you don't know what's happening. I've seen it coming for a long time now. Titty bars are changing. These chains, they sometimes run three, four hundred tits out of one head office. They got tits in Houston, tits in Dallas, tits in Norleans. They got *health plans,* Joe Bob. Those girls get their garbonzas checked, free of charge, three times a year. They got day-care nurseries at ever tit joint in San Antone. How we gonna compete with that?"

"Rhett, what are you saying? This is Chez Highway 290. This is where the whole thing started. We got *bestiality,* for Chrissakes."

"They got it, too. Everybody's got bestiality now. How long did you think we could keep it for ourselves?"

"I still say that don't mean José dumped me for a chain contract."

"Don't blame her, Joe Bob. These agents, they prey on tits like hers. You said yourself all she had was a couple of 32s, and how much longer can her tadpole muscles hold out? She's gotta make it while she can. She can't sit around the goat ranch all day long."

"But I had no idea."

"Course you didn't. The husband's always the last to know."

For a while I tried to hold things together at the club, holding auditions, putting on a few shows, but my heart wasn't in it after José's tits left. I started drinking heavily at lunch, downing Tequila shooters all afternoon. I was rapidly losing my will to live. And then, miraculously, on March 23, 1967, I was saved a second time.

It started out like any other day. I arrived at the shed around 11 and started planning the music for that night. In fact, I think it was the night we introduced our "Age of Aquarius" production number for the first time, with fifteen girls in open-tit body stockings, being relevant.

About 12:30 Rhett came and got me and said there was about thirty women milling around outside the club, carrying signs with stuff on em like "Stop Sexism Now," and "Half the Human Race Enslaved by Pornography," and other stuff that didn't make sense. So, even though it wasn't a Monday, I said, "Bring em on in and have em line up on the dance floor."

And so Rhett went out and got em and brought em in for cattle call.

I'm telling you, these must of been the grand prize winners of 1967 International Ugly Rama, cause I've never seen such a herd of porkers in my life. But everbody gets an equal shot at Chez Highway 290, and so I yelled, "Okay, everbody show me your titties."

Nobody made a move, so I said, "Excuse me, but you all need to remove your blouses at this time."

The ugliest one of all, a bimbo by the name of Margaret Katiski-Fisher, strutted up front in her sandals and said, "Is your name Briggs?"

And I said, "No, it's *Mister* Briggs. Is your name Jane Fonda?"

"Briggs," she said, "we are here to protest the continued existence of your nightclub, where each night women are paraded around like cattle to be gawked at by jerks who can't relate to women except as inanimate sex objects."

"That's correct."

"We are *appalled* at the way you advertise the female breast as some form of voyeuristic performance."

"Please say that again."

"We are *appalled* at the way you use the female breast for cheap, vicarious sexual thrill."

"You mean titties?"

"I want to ask you a question, Mr. Briggs. Do you find the traffic in naked women to be a worthwhile use of your energy?"

"Not really."

"I notice you're smiling. Do you find the female breast to be funny?"

"Unfortunately, most tits are funny, yes."

"Well, we do *not* think the subject is funny."

"Really? You wanna show me your tits?"

"Mr. Briggs, you can joke about this all you want, but we're here to demand that you close your nightclub, as it's a disgrace and a humiliation to women everywhere, to women as a class, to women as a sex, and to women as feeling human beings."

"Feeling human beans?"

"Women will no longer be the passive targets of male aggression."

"Okay," I said.

"Okay what?"

"Okay, you're right."

"What are we right about?"

"You're right that tits aren't very interesting anymore," I told her, "and the big titty-bar chains are running me out anyhow, and so okay."

"What?"

"I'll close her down."

"What?"

"I was kind of sick of the place anyhow. Time to move on. Tits are a dime a dozen these days."

"What?"

"I never thought about just shutting up shop till you brought it up. You're right."

"You mean you're gonna close?"

"I'll close her down tonight."

"Is this something you already planned before we came in?"

"No, but I have to tell you, if you gals are any example of the kind of tits on the market these days, I'm closing just in the nick of time."

And I'll tell you something about that lady with the three names: she never did even give me a thank you or nothing. She said close her down, I closed her down. But that's how the feminine movement is. I didn't know it at the time, but that was my very first run-in with the National Organization of Bimbos. They were on my case then, and they're on my case now, twenty-one years later. I don't care what I do, they're on my case.

I'm not a violent kind of guy. I think I need to point this out because one time the National Organization of Bimbos accused me of "glorifying violence toward women" and "contributing to an atmosphere of hatred in this country." Now you may think after they attacked me like that, I might of went down to Handy Dan's hardware and picked up an industrial-model Black & Decker and turned Gloria Steinem's face into homemade lasagna. Or you may think, after having my integrity destroyed by these bimbos, I might of grabbed the nearest thirty-aught-six and air-conditioned a few upper torsos. Or maybe you just think I should of grabbed a few of em and slapped em up side of the head a few times and then made em get down on their hands and knees like dogs and bark for mercy.

Well, you'll be surprised to learn I didn't do none of that. I did the civilized thing. I did the respectable thing. I did the *non-violent* thing.

I challenged em all to a nude mud-wrestling match.

And I think it says something about the sincerity of the feminine movement in this country of ours that none of em has ever accepted the offer.

I would like to make it clear right now that I am violently opposed to mass murder in America, including the mass murder of most women.

I'm probly gonna need a whole chapter to give you my opinion of the National Organization of Bimbos, but in the meantime I'd just like to tell you one thing they say about me. They say that geeks and weirdos read my column, "Joe Bob Goes to the Drive-In," all the time. Sickos, psychos, and creepolas. The kind of people who live in Oakland, California. And then these individuals learn how to commit multiple psycho murders and then they go out and rape little girls on their way to school and bomb the public library and turn their mothers into mincemeat pie.

Okay, okay, so maybe I've caused one or two mass murders. But *most of the time* I have a completely harmless, peace-loving, God-fearing syndicated column that makes me an extra eighty bucks a week. I'll tell you how I know this is true. Remember *Maniac,* the flick about the Jonestown graduate who goes around sticking farm implements through people? Everbody has their favorite scene in that movie. I guess mine is the one where the bimbo and her boyfriend go out to the lover's lane and start making out, and while they're distracted, the maniac jumps up on the hood with a double-barrel shotgun and fires that mother through the windshield, in slow motion, and blows the boyfriend's head into about 1,600 pieces while the stump between his shoulders keeps shooting blood all over the girl. Okay, now here's my point. It's been five years since that flick came out, and there is not *one reported incident* of somebody's head being blown off by a double-barrel shotgun fired through a windshield by a maniac standing on a car hood watching a bimbo scarf up some French kisses. And I think this is fairly obvious evidence that the mass murderers who regularly read "Joe Bob Goes to the Drive-In" do *not* imitate scenes described in the column proper.

But that's the National Organization of Bimbos for you. Always *distorting* the truth for sensationalism. It makes me so depressed that I'm gonna stop this chapter right now and send it off to New York and see if they'll gimme my money and let me stop writing about the history of the world, cause frankly I'm getting embarrassed talking about myself like this. Normally I never talk about myself, but you know, people come up all the time and say, "Hey, Joe Bob, how'd you get so goddamn famous?" And you just can't let em down.

So what was this chapter about anyhow? Oh yeah. The feminists are right about one thing:

It's not the size of a woman's breasts that makes her what she is. It's whether she can make those titties stand up and do tricks or not.

9

The Search for José

I did a lot of crazy things to try to forget José. I counted backwards from the number 12,000. That didn't work. I wore burlap underwear. And when it got the worst, late at night, when I started to have the exploding-bazooma nightmares, I even thought about the ultimate release. Yep, I considered it. I'm not proud to say it, but I considered tying a two-by-four to my rear end and hiding in a lumber pile until I was nailed to death as part of a Century 21 Flair home. It didn't work, though.

I was so depressed I couldn't even do *that* right.

Finally, I decided to quit moonin around the trailer house and do something about it. So I went out to the tool shed, rousted Bobo Rodriguez out of his deep "la beera"-induced slumber, and said, "Bobo, we're gonna go find José. I know she still loves me."

And Bobo, he didn't question it or nothin, he just shook it off, threw a couple mufflers over his right shoulder, pulled a fistful of hair out of his chest like he does every morning, and went out back to get the Merc fired up for wife-huntin. By the time I got in the car, he had it purring like a kitten in a trash compacter.

"Bobo," I said, "bus station."

And Bobo tore off for the Greyhound station over in Ozona where José was last seen.

When we got there, I went inside and discussed my situation with the ticket agent, a weasel-face little guy name of Leon Turley.

"Leon, as you know, I'm the famous pornographer and smut merchant Joe Bob Briggs."

"Say that again," Leon said.

"Leon, you know I own a titty bar, right?"

"I thought you closed her down."

"I did close her down. But you know that I have a certain *clout* in this area due to my influence in the Texas Legislature."

"You don't say."

"And so I want you to hear me, Leon, this is *very* important what I'm gonna tell you."

"Okay."

"Leon, my wife come into this bus station, *your* bus station, and committed an unlawful act against the laws of the state of Texas."

Leon got an expression on his face like somebody was about to rub jelly on his stomach.

"What happened was, she *left* me, Leon. Which, as you know, is a direct violation of the husband-wife eternal-happiness laws we brought over from Spain that also says you can shoot any booger that diddles your wife out of wedlock. So what we got here, Leon, is my wife is a known criminal."

"I'm sorry to hear it, Joe Bob."

"Well, everbody is. Now, what we need from you, Leon, is we need to know just exactly where José went when she come down here last week and bought a bus ticket."

"Sorry, Joe Bob, but the company won't let me give that out, and also it'd be too hard to figure out."

"Leon, I'd like to donate two bucks to your favorite charity. Here it is right here."

"I guess they wouldn't mind if it was a police matter."

"It is, Leon, it's a police matter. And besides that, Leon, I'd like to give you three *more* dollars for your favorite underprivileged child or else your church or else something else that I can write off on my taxes."

And so that's basically what happened, and it ended up costin me *five bucks* just to find out that my wife took the *east* bus that goes all the way to New York City if you have a hunnerd bucks and healthy hemorrhoids.

So that was it—that's all I knew. The only woman I ever loved, lost somewhere between Ozona and New York City, all alone, nursing her chest back to health. It was enough to make you sick.

For the next month all Bobo and me did was search for José. We checked in Sonora, Junction, Kerrville, San Antone, San Marcos, Austin, and then San Marcos again, cause they have a diving pig on display there and I promised I'd take Bobo back to see it if he went on to Austin with me.

We checked the bus stations, the hotels, the titty bars, the bestiality bars, and the private apartments of 34 state legislators. No José. Ever once in a while we thought we had a lead. Like somebody would say, "Oh yeah, little skinny girl with charbroil marks on her nipples? I think I do remember her. Joey Heatherton page-boy haircut? Chartreuse pants suit? Carried a duffel bag marked '22nd Airborne'? Half-moons under each armpit? She was through here. Tried to sell me a set of World Books."

"That's her! It must be! Her life's ambition was to go into World Book sales! What did she say?"

"She said I really ought to be thinking about the preparation of my children for a college education, and getting them the reference materials they need."

"Not about the World Book! Where'd she say she was going?"

"She didn't."

"What do you mean? She must have left some clue."

"Well, there was one thing."

"Yeah?"

"She said she would never again pay good money to see that diving pig."

Time after time, we ran across the same information. José was *not in San Marcos, Texas.* Slowly, step by step, we were narrowing down the possibilities. She was somewhere *outside of* San Marcos, but *inside* the United States. The reason I know this is I happen to know you can't buy World Book in Mexico.

It was still kind of discouraging, though, to know that no matter where we looked or how we looked, a gal in World Book sales is gonna be all over the lot. Waco this week, Corsicana next week, there just hardly isn't any rhyme nor reason to it.

And then we got our first breakthrough:

The Diner's Club bills started comin in.

There's a lot of special skills you pick up when you work in a titty bar all your adult life like José did, and one of em is how to charge on Diner's Club. Diner's Club is the only credit card in existence that'll take on a goat-ranch titty-rama as a client. José was one of the best Diner's Club gals we had. Before the guy could get the words "pink near-champagne" out of his mouth, José had the wallet out, the card in the kathumpa machine, and the total amount of 25 bucks filled out at the bottom. It was knowledge she was using to her advantage now, as she hauled her hiney all over creation with a set of World Books in the backseat. I returned to the ranch to study the evidence.

The Diner's Club envelope weighed in at 17 pounds and had a special notice attached that said, "Dear Valued Account Holder," which means, of course, they're ready to sue you from here to Nome, Alaska. I didn't even care about that, though. All I could think about, night and day,

day and night, was José's lost titties. Sometimes I'd even panic. I was *forgetting what her chest looked like.* I'd try to recall it to memory, search out all of its two features, and try to put it back together in my mind. But it was a fading memory, like breast reduction surgery.

Slowly I poured out the 374 Diner's Club receipts on my desk, hoping for some clue, some sign, some trail of paper that I could waste the next three, four months on. But everthing went in circles:

April 26, Teepee Lodge, Alice, Texas, $21.46.

April 29, Pig Pen Restaurant, Eagle Pass, $8.74.

May 3, Ralph the Diving Pig Show, San Marcos, $2.00. (So we were *right* about her route. My heart started moonwalkin.)

May 17, Striper Fishing Derby, Lake Texoma, Denison, Texas, $35.00.

May 18, Ranger Bob's Buffalo Courts, Ardmore, Oklahoma, $27.73.

And then, suddenly, it hit me like a nine-ton hydraulic back-hoe dropped off a football stadium.

It was too much money!

It was too much money for ONE PERSON!

"This is too much money," I said to Bobo, kicking him in the stomach and causing him to stop snoring.

"Humpa humpa?" he mumbled.

"Bobo, look at this! Look at this! I can't believe it!"

And I took one of the receipts out of my pocket with trembling hands, and I handed it over to him, and it looked like this:

07854389911

J.B. Briggs

MAY 22, 1967

Retailer: Arbuckle's House of Incredibly Expensive Silk Shirts

         610 W. Jackson Street

         Hugo, Oklahoma

Items:	2 aquamarine shts	$23.00
	1 canary yellow sht	16.75
	1 "Sinatra" fedora	28.20
	6 pr. sox	3.25
	1 Arbuckle's three-year lunar calendar	FREE
TOTAL PURCHASE		$71.20
	plus 2 Schrafft's dinner mints	.02
TOTAL		*71.22*

"Join our Mister Silkworm Club. You are now eligible for *712* bonus points."

"Don't forget us for funeral and wedding needs!"

Authorized signature: Joyce Karnes-Briggs

I don't know which it was that got to me more. Was it the "Joyce Karnes-Briggs," like she was workin her way back to her name before I made her world famous? Or was it the dinner mints?

The dinner mints were too depressin. I couldn't get the dinner mints out of my mind. There they were, standing next to the cash register in Hugo, Oklahoma, with José stackin silk shirts on a glass-top counter and sayin somethin in her Kewpie-doll voice like "Oh, I'd *love* a Schrafft's, wouldn't you?" and then rippin the tinfoil off a couple of em and poppin one into *his* mouth.

With *my money!*

Bobo looked at the receipt and asked me if he could have the free calendar.

Sometimes your friends can make you lonely.

For the next six hours, I just sat there in front of the Motorola, starin at the PBA Tour, followed by Albanian ice skating, professional steer kissing from Oklahoma City (*Oklahoma City!* I couldn't even bear to hear the *word* "Oklahoma"), and "Goat Country Reporter," the most popular program in that part of West Texas where this guy goes out in a van and interviews old farts sitting around playin dominoes in public. But today I didn't even *learn* anything from "Goat Country Reporter." All my thoughts were on José, José, only on José.

I wanted to kill her to prove my love.

Along about nine or ten o'clock that night, I kicked Bobo out of the trailer cause I wanted to be totally alone with myself, and then I pulled out the Diner's Club envelope again and I started going through it, from front to back, and I stayed up all night long and all Sunday morning and halfway through Sunday afternoon studying on it and trying to figure out exactly what I was gonna do. First I stacked all the bills in piles by states, but that didn't work cause these two *lovebirds* kept crossing state lines back and forth. So then I put it in order accordin to date, and that was a little bit better, cause I could get out the Rand McNally and trace their route with a Crayola, but it still had so many zigzags on it that it looked like Phil Donahue's brain scan. And then, finally, about seventeen hours after I started, I saw a line on one of the receipts that brought me up short. In fact, it brought me up about three-foot-nine.

Right there, in black and white, it said "7 Beanee Weenee, $1.40."

My brain went blank. I froze. My eyeballs turned over six times. My shirt shrank three sizes. I could feel blackness on the inside of my right big toe.

I knew.

It was all clear to me.

It was Rhett Judas Beavers.

10

The Beanee Weenee Trail

It seemed like all clues led to Hugo, Oklahoma. Whatever happened, however it happened, why it happened, whose disgusting little motel room it happened in, one thing was certain. It happened in the Hugo city limits.

This time I didn't take Bobo. This time I was determined to do it alone, and I didn't want Bobo to have to look at what I was about to do. I downed a 12-pack of Old Milwaukee Tall Boys and hit the road north. I stopped for a half gallon of coffee in San Angelo, but other than that I kept it on the floorboard, flattened three armadillos crossin the highway and got a big old tumbleweed stuck on the front grille that was in there so thick I was still findin pieces of it a year later. About twenty miles past Abilene it kicked up a dust storm and wiped out three, four elementary schools, but I didn't even notice. I just kept haulin, like Robert Mitchum in *Thunder Road,* and I didn't fag out till about 5 in the A.M. when I rolled into Wichita Falls and found a bed at the Alpine Comfort Rest Courts for five bucks. I picked up about three hours shut-eye, then crossed the Red River up at Waurika, Oklahoma, where the dirt turns candy-apple red, and then cut over on U.S. 70 through Ardmore and Durant and threw a rod outside Boswell on account of they didn't have any paving for about three miles through there, and by the time they got it fixed and I limped into Hugo, it was a full 26 hours trip I made.

I was real careful how I eased the Merc into Hugo, so I didn't arouse any suspicions. I found a place just outside town, called the Cotton Pickins Motel, owned by the Pickins family of Lawton, Oklahoma, except on the wife's side where they were all from Tahlequah till they got kicked out for paintin pig's hineys on the Babtist Church. If you ever get up to Hugo, you'll recognize the Cotton Pickins Motel by the 104-year-old Indian that sits out front of the office wearin a floppy felt hat and leather pants and the "Trail of Tears" etched into every line on his weathered face. His name is Boris, and he gets two bucks an hour to sit out there. It's a deal the Oklahoma Tourist Commission come up with, to spread the old Indians around closer to the main east-west highways. Boris also sells Amway products out of his station wagon.

For about two days after I got to Hugo I just sorta sized up the situation by sleepin and sightseeing. Just me, Room 105 at the Cotton Pickins Motel, a black-and-white Zenith with a big ole grease spot on the top of it where I put the Kentucky Fried Chicken bag, and a little gal named Fran that used to come by and change the towels and make King, her German shepherd, stop pissin in the pool, and say stuff life, "You checkin out?" Fran and me had many great conversations, specially on the days when I'd answer her: "Nope." The only sightseein is out on Hugo Lake, where you can rent you an Evinrude and go out and club froggies to death in the swamps.

I was bidin my time, makin my plan. Some days I'd just lay on the sheets all day long, with my hands behind my head, staring at the yellow bulb with the chain, and wondering why the chain keeps swinging all the time when nobody's messin with it. On other days, I'd look at the Co-Cola bottle opener over by the sink and wonder why they

don't put bottle openers in regular trailer houses, just in
motels. I had a lot of interesting thoughts during this
period of my life. But most days I'd plan exactly what I
was gonna do to Rhett and Jo . . . Jo . . . I couldn't
hardly say her name anymore . . . what I was gonna do
to the two Dirty Diddlin Champeens of the Known Universe whenever I caught em at it. One thing I was gonna
do—I had this part of it all planned out—is I was gonna
confiscate ever single silk shirt I could get my hands on.
Then I was gonna take em outside and soak em in the gas
tank and wrap em around a Chinese bottle rocket and
play "Pin the Molotov Cocktail on the Nekkid Flesh" until
they blew several city blocks into the ozone. But mostly I
kept thinkin, "I gotta get that Diner's Club card back."
That thing was costin me a *fortune.*

Like I say, I bided awhile.

Then I got cleaned up one morning and made my
move. I put on my best set of Amarillo Slim wrangler wear
and headed for Jackson Street and the scene of the crime:
Arbuckle's House of Incredibly Expensive Silk Shirts.

It wasn't much to look at—just a bunch of pre-fab-crete
grey walls with a fresh coat of grey paint on em. They had
a sign hanging on a pole out front that said "Arbuckle's" in
curvy writing, like it was done by a Hawaiian homo. Underneath the sign was a Cherokee Indian sittin "squaw-
style" and frowning with the pain of a century of tragic
fire-water consumption. I pulled back the screen door and
looked in, and as soon as I did, I could see what kind of
perversion I was dealing with. Row after row, rack after
rack, all you could see through this entire store—and it
was at least eight, ten feet wide—was silk, silk, silk. You'd
think the PLO was having a convention there was so
many shiny silk shirts in there. I almost needed a set of
sunglasses just to get by the purple ones, but once I
wedged myself into a corner where the glare was cut

down, I could see Arbuckle, settin on a stool behind the cash register, squinting his eyes so he could read the *Hugo Daily Bleeder,* devoted to the pig industry in that part of the country.

Arbuckle was about five-five and weighed 270 and had curly white hair on top of a head that looked like the *National Geographic* map of the Rocky Mountains. I judged him for a cigar smoker—either that or his lips were used for chinchilla breeding. I never could stand cigar smokers, specially the ones that made squishy noises on the end that was real wet and gooey. That's what Arbuckle was doing, using one end of his cigar like it was a Wet 'n' Wild Amusement Park water slide. Anyhow, he never did look up from the *Bleeder,* just let me moon around the store like I knew what I was doing.

I didn't wanna look suspicious, so I picked up a magenta silk shirt with double safari pockets on it, took it up to the counter, and said, "Excuse me."

Arbuckle rustled his paper a little bit, looked over the top of it, and said, "Fourteen."

"Wha'd you say?"

"Fourteen bucks. Shirt's fourteen bucks."

And he went back to reading the *Bleeder.*

"Oh, I didn't want *this* shirt," I told him. "I wouldn't use *this* shirt for storing rat doo-doo."

I thought I'd try to loosen him up a little bit with that remark, but he kept on reading.

"Actually," I told him, "I want something a *whole lot* more expensive than this shirt."

He looked over the paper again.

"I want something like . . ." I was trying to remember what it was on the receipt, but it wouldn't come to me. Arbuckle kept staring at me.

"I want something like one of them Sinatra doohickeys."

"Fedora?"

"Right," I said. "Sinatra fedora. I *hear* they're about 28, 29 dollars."

"Twenty-seven with the shirt." Arbuckle put the paper down. "You're the second guy in two weeks wanted one of them."

"Are you kiddin me? I thought everbody wanted one."

Arbuckle licked his cigar, flung 30, 40 pounds of ashes into the ashtray, and started to say something. He picked up the paper again.

"I thought Hugo was where they had the Sinatra Fedora *Festival!*"

Of course, this was a complete lie. Everbody knew the Sinatra Fedora Festival was in Tahlequah, but I had to get the guy to talking.

"Fiddle festival's about all we have in Hugo," he said. "All white people have, anyhow."

"That's too bad. I was hoping to go to the festival this year and do some serious fedora trading. Like this one you got right here" (I pulled a hat off the display case) "it's *all right,* but watch this."

I put it on my head and pulled the brim down close over my eyebrows.

"You see that? Look at my face."

Arbuckle looked at me.

"Sinatra? Durante? Jackie Gleason when he was real fat in *Requiem for a Heavyweight?*"

Arbuckle got a look on his face like a zoo-monkey going on the Johnny Carson show.

"No!" I yelled at him. "It don't look like Sinatra. It don't look like Gleason. And it sure don't look like Durante. You know what it looks like?"

Arbuckle got a look on his face like a zoo-monkey going on *The Dick Cavett Show.*

"It looks like grape jelly on a biscuit! Would you wear

grape jelly on *your* head? I didn't think so. What'd you do, *sell* all the *decent* Sinatra fedoras?"

Arbuckle still didn't say nothing at first.He closed the *Bleeder,* folded it in half, and laid it carefully beside his cash register. He took the dripping cigar out of his mouth and stubbed it out on a scale replica of the famous teepee burned up by drunk cavalry soldiers in 1874 at the Battle of The Runs. Then Arbuckle squinted his little red rat-eyes at me and he said, "I know why you're here."

I tried to interrupt him to say that I was on his premises for no other reason except to purchase the finest quality Sinatra fedora available on the open market, but he wouldn't let me.

"I know why you're here. You're here because of them two that were in here a couple weeks ago dressing their-selves up like rainbow trout. Your name is Joe Bob Briggs, I bet. I noticed it on their Diner's Club, even asked em about it, sized up the situation, knew there was probly a husband out in Guymon or wherever you're from."

"West Texas."

"West Texas. Whatever. And I tell you what, Mister, you just might as well give up on the deal. She's no damn good. She was hangin on him like dirt on a rat potty. She paraded her little mini-skirt in here like she was sellin thighs and the first thing out of her mouth was 'Don't you think this handsome man here needs some silk on his aching body?' That's what she called it—his *aching* body. Now it's none of my business one way or the other. I sell shirts. People can wear the shirts or tie em on their pecker, I don't care. But the way she said it, I don't know, I just said to myself, 'Arbuckle, they're trouble. Sell em what they want, get em on their way. Trouble. Nothin but trouble.' That's what I said to myself right away, and then I took a good look at the guy—scrawny guy, sickly-looking, like he's been in the Mitch Miller Singers too long, got the goatee and everthing—and I start thinkin to myself 'Hippies in Hugo.' Here we think we're safe, and what happens. Hippies show up here to burn down the bowling alley. And so then I'm *really* ready to get em out of here and back on the highway, only they decide they need *two hours* to look at shirts. They must of tried on 50, 60 shirts, and there wasn't but three of em that ever fit him, and two of them was the identical color. And all the time they're tryin em on, *she's* going back in the tryout room with him, saying stuff like 'Oh, *that's* a good one,' and 'That's a *good* one,' and giggling a lot and if you ask me they was doing more back there than just trying on shirts, but then I'm not the kinda guy that's gonna go back there and look in on people in their privacy because, let's face it, I can get sued."

Arbuckle leaned over the counter. His beady eyes were actually gettin a little bigger as he told the story.

"But here's the weird part. Finally we get all the funny business over with, and what do you think the guy wants to do?"

I shook my head. I was still trying to figure out what a rat potty is.

"Go ahead, guess what he wanted to do?"

There was so many things I did *not* wanna think about at this time that I said, "No, I can't. I might break something."

"The guy wants to pay in Mexican money. He wants to give me some greasebacks. And you know where he's *got* this money? He's carryin it around in a *suitcase.* He opens it up for me, and I can see he's got in there maybe 270 billion pesos, which in American money is about, I don't know, 50, 60 dollars. And so I say, 'No way I'm taking that stuff,' and so *she* whips out the Diner's Club, and right away I'm suspicious. Right away I'm saying this Diner's Club didn't come in the mail one day. And so I ask her for

some Eye-Dee. And she comes up with the Eye-Dee, it says her name's Briggs on the license and everthing, and so I let her go on and charge it cause, hey, 70 bucks *is* 70 bucks, it don't pay to be too picky. But I guess what you come here to find out is what happened after they left, right?"

I was now so totally confused that I tried to remember just why I *had* come here in the first place.

"Well." Arbuckle leaned way over the counter and whispered for no reason. "I happen to *know* where they went. They made the mistake of talking to Dexter."

"Dexter?"

"Didn't you meet Dexter? He's the Indian sittin out front."

"The one frowning with the pain of a century of tragic fire-water consumption etched on his face?"

"Right. I pay for ever tragic line, too. They start blabbin to Dexter on the way out, and you know what he finds out? He finds out that they're gettin all dressed up for the big bass tournament at Lake Quapaw. Dexter finds out their whole life story, how they travel around selling World Books at bass tournaments and making big money on commissions. And you know what? I guess the last laugh's on me, cause Dexter even found out about the suitcase full of billions of pesos. You know how they got all those pesos?"

"No," I said edgewise.

"The last bass tournament they went to was down in Mexico. Lake Titicaca or something."

I happen to know that the World Book is *not* sold in Mexico, but I held my peace.

"And that's all I know," said Arbuckle. "None of my damn business. I'm not getting involved in it."

"Thanks," I said, wondering what in hell I was gonna do

with a Sinatra fedora now that I wanted to get the heck
out. "What do I owe you?"

"Nothin," Arbuckle said. "Put the hat back and have a
dinner mint."

My insides turned to seafood gumbo when he said "dinner mint." I had to know.

"Uh, Mr. Arbuckle, I noticed on the Diner's Club receipt that they purchased two Schrafft's dinner mints
from this bowl on your counter."

"Did they?" Arbuckle said absent-mindedly.

"I guess there wouldn't be any significance to that,
would there?"

"I guess not."

Arbuckle started reading the *Bleeder* again and I
turned to go.

"The only thing it probly means," he said, "is that
they're diddlin each other's brains out."

On my way to the car, I stopped and kicked several
more permanent etchings of anguish into Dexter's face. It
made me feel a little better.

11

Bass Fishin in America

I didn't have much time, but I finally had a bead on her. If I was gonna be able to hunt down José, manipulate her into comin back to me, tear up all her credit cards, and beat the sofa stuffin out of Rhett Beavers, then I only had about forty-eight hours to get ready. That was all the time left before the entry deadline at the 8th Annual Lake Quapaw Bass Tournament and Recreational Vehicle Rally over by Stuttgart, Arkansas, which had got so popular by this time that they were expectin 2,000 fishermen includin the entire Fellowship of Christian Bass Fisherman of Tupelo, Mississippi, who were comin up in a Winnebago convoy. A lot of people might of turned back if they heard that, thinkin "No way I'm gonna be able to fish my limit with that many jerks in bass boats out there," but that's the person that ain't never seen Lake Quapaw. Lake Quapaw's so thick with bass that as soon as you open up your lure box, three or four bass generally jump up into the boat and commit suicide.

Anyhow, I didn't give a flip about catchin no bass. I was only intersted in catchin José. And so I had to have a plan. I wasn't gonna be satisfied with just *findin* her. All that would mean is I go up to her like a Pekinese dog that got whupped with a two-by-four and ask her if she'll forgive me, and frankly I didn't wanna give her the satisfaction, the way I was feeling. No, my wife was suspected of committin a sexual felony in *at least* two other states besides Texas, and I strongly suspected she'd been diddlin in Louisiana as well, and so I figured she had to be trussed up like a pig and hauled back to justice.

I was headed out of Hugo by nightfall and pointed towards Little Rock even though I knew I'd have to cross through the Ouachita Mountains in the dark and that meant that I'd probly be smashed into bacon bits by the first weasel haulin a trailer that jack-knifed on a downslip. In the Arkansas mountains they're so used to this that they don't even put it in the paper unless there's at least seven or eight dead pre-schoolers or else somebody famous dies, like Orville Stubbs, coach of the University of Arkansas Razorback football freshman team, the "Piglets," who died just one year earlier on State Highway 84 outside of Umpire, Arkansas, where the slope got so steep his brakes started singing the high parts on the *Bee Gees Greatest Hits* album and then a farmer named Clete made a left out of his cattle gate and basically finished the chorus for him. They found parts of Orville Stubbs clear over in Pike County, which was actually very fortunate, cause at the time Orville was such a famous individual that the Pike County Quorum Court passed a formal resolution askin that they be allowed to keep a small part of Orville for permanent burial on the Pike County Courthouse grounds, where they erected a small monument to the 1969 Piglets, who were 6 and 1 in conference play and would of won that other game, too, except Texas A&M kicked a field goal with two seconds left that everbody in the state of Arkansas agrees did *not* go through the uprights, it was actually a full foot wide, and so having Orville partially buried on your courthouse grounds was something of an honor and I think you can see why *his* particular grisly highway death in the Ouachitas did result in a two-column photo on page 3 of the *Caddo Gap Arkansianan*. But if I was to die—this was back in the years before I was world famous—then all there'd be is a little grease spot on the pavement.

Anyhow, I gunned it on up through Antlers, Oklahoma, and across to Kiamichi and Big Cedar where you start to get into the piney woods and slammed into Mena, Arkansas, about ten o'clock and kept climbin and weavin and watchin the forty-foot pines whiz by and get brown stuff all over the hood, and I guess God must of been blessin me on my mission of vengeance that night, cause I only had one close call and that was from an oncoming wood-paneled station wagon that had one front headlight out and so it was coming straight at me down *my* side of the road *on purpose* so I'd *know* he had the front light out. This is what you call your Arkansas family of first-cousin marriages. I went ahead and took the ditch and then beat his back fender in with a stick to teach him not to do that no more.

I pulled into Little Rock about 3:30 in the A.M., but I couldn't be waitin around to get started. I went straight to Adams Field, also known as the Little Rock International Airport, except to people who live there, who call it Adams Field, and then as I sneaked past the guy that's supposed to take your money for parking, I *prayed* to God that it was still there. If it wasn't there, I didn't know what I was gonna do. Probly would of killed myself that very night. Probly would of slunk over to the Arkansas River bridge, picked out a brown gooey place, and jumped in there with all the alligator gar and nucular waste. But the Big Guy reached down with his hand that night and saved my hiney again. Cause as soon as I turned the corner down by the deserted Arkansairways counter, I could see the dark shape of it still sittin there in front of the McBurger Hut Airport Restaurant. It was on permanent display, like a scientific exhibition for tourists. I knew I was meant to have it. It was a 235-horsepower double-seated 22-foot Astroturf-covered attack-prow Bass Master. It was the only weapon I was gonna need.

I don't know how long I stood there lookin at it. It was like one of them scenes in the Old Testament where the prophet sees a vision and so all his gizzards start twirlin around and the world thinks he's crazy and to show em he's not he has to point at the ground and make it crack open and swallow up a couple hunnerd of em. That's how I felt at that moment. I felt like I could point at the linoleum in that airport and it would just open right up and start spittin bass up out of the earth.

They had a little sign by the side of the boat:

"Available only through Razorback Marine, 3742 New Benton Highway, Jack Davis, resident Bass Master"

When the sun came up, I was already sittin out front of the shop, ready to deal.

The way I recognized Jack Davis right away as a resident bass master is he showed up wearin a canary-yellow jump suit, a cushioned vest that had patches all over the back, a white felt hat that sat way back on his head like it was ceemented to the back of his neck, and also he looked like a man that'd been sittin in a bass boat for most of the last forty years. Bass masters always have names like Jack Davis. You ever hear of a guy name of somethin like Marcello Vitulli or Sigfried Piotrowski, forget it, he ain't a bass master. Bill Williams—*that's* a bass master. Jimmy Houston—bass master. Richard Mann—definite bass master. These guys with two many vowels in their names catch stuff like salmon and trout and sushi and live up in Seattle. Jack Davis was the ultimate bass master.

"Hello," he said as he jumped out of his combination camper/trailer/pickup/canoe rental office and extended his gloved hand. "Jack Davis, Bass Master."

"I know," I told him. "I'm Joe Bob Briggs and I wanna do some fishin this weekend."

"Sorry, this is Quapaw weekend. All booked up. Can't help you."

"I'm the world's wealthiest pornographer from West Texas and I'm prepared to finance you on the bass-fishin tour for one entire year and also I'll buy a Bass Master 9000 like the one in the airport and a monster RV from your company and all you got to do is spend one day with me catchin bass."

Jack Davis eyed me up one side and down the other.

"Cash?" he said.

"Cash."

"Anything illegal?" he asked.

"I'm gonna kidnap my wife and maybe murder one of my best friends."

"It's a deal."

That's the kind of guy Jack Davis was. He had total bass integrity.

We retired to the Razorback Marine sales office for a conference. And, of course, the rest is history.

12

True Love in Arkansas

At 5 A.M., on the morning of July 3, 1967, somethin emerged from the underbrush surrounding Lake Quapaw, Arkansas, that had never been seen before in the recorded history of recreational vehicles. What it was, technically, was a converted Born Free Wanderlodge with a Detroit Diesel 8V-92, galvanized steel underbelly, black-tinted windows, United States Marine Corps salvage personnel-carrier pontoons hooked on over each wheel well, a 300-gallon high-octane propulsion fuel tank, a sign on the side that said "Bass Monster," and a Quasar/Sharp microwave oven, which actually is standard on all Born Free Wanderlodges anyway. From what I know, this is the first fully amphibious RV with enough firepower to invade Communist Russia. But what folks did *not* know about the Bass Monster is the secret compartment that flopped out the back of it, like a baby diaper escape hatch, where we had secretly concealed the 950-horse double-decker Super Bass Master competition boat, Jim Davis at the controls. The whole rig, Bass Monster, Bass Master, and microwave, cost me $455,000, which in 1967 money was approximately $455,000. In other words, my whole life's savings, all the money I'd made off titties in my entire life. José didn't know it yet, but it was all for her.

Like I say, Jim and me set the Bass Monster on the

water at 5 A.M., which gave me about two hours to check gauges, take sonar readings, and heat up 7-Eleven frozen burritos in the microwave. I had me one of them Largemouth A-100 fish-findin depth-sounders with the 18-color computer screen—you know, everbody's got one of em now, so it's no big deal, but in 1967 this was the bass boat of the future—and then on top of that I had a high-powered telescope, a periscope, a high-powered lake police escape boat, a queen-size bed, and three U.S. Army issue LAW one-shot rocket-launched anti-tank weapons. I think you're beginning to see by now just how truly I did love José.

The guy I hired to actually drive the Bass Monster was Yakohira Mishima, who I hired cause he told me he was a kamikaze pilot in World War II, but Jim Davis said he was a little suspicious of him due to his resemblance to Homer Withers, who used to live five miles down the road in Brummitt, Arkansas, but nobody'd seen him in fifteen years and they thought it was cause he'd gone up to Minnesota and shot eighteen members of his family and then snuck back down to Arkansas after disguisin hisself as a Japaheeno veteran. I didn't think anybody would go to that much trouble just to kill his family, but Yakohira *was* six-foot-three and so I thought it might have a chance of being true. Anyhow, I said to Jim, "Jim, we ain't hirin choir boys on this mission."

And Jim said, "We ain't?"

Yakohira eased the Bass Monster down into the lake that morning and all of a sudden we were swimmin in tall scum. Very first thing happened is Jim's trollin blade got all gummed up with some elephant weed or whatever it was they got growin in that lake, and Jim had to jump down in the water and try to get her workin again before the mosquitoes ate his elbow off. While he was doing that, I scanned the horizon, searching for José and her partner in slime. I knew they'd be early out on the lake, probly *cheatin* their way through the tournament, probly tryin to sneak frozen bass into the water so they could win the $2,000 trip to Acapulco and diddle each other some more. All I saw this mornin, though, was a few scrawny ducks, a couple of old oil-rig platforms where somebody started drillin back in 67 and then give up cause all he struck was quartz-crystal souvenir paperweights, and three or four legitimate bassers wearin orange lifejackets, buzzin around each other like Hell's Angels, cuttin donuts, givin it the thumbs-up ever time they whizzed by, so they could go home that night and tell the wife what macho bass-fishin fools they were.

Jim finally got the trollin blade ungummed, and just when he popped back up inside the Bass Monster, a huge pink blip in the shape of Dino the Dinosaur showed up on the sonar trackin screen. It kept bobbin in the water, like Dino was about to sprout wings, and so I called out for Jim to scope it out with me.

"Yo!" Jim said as he came up to the screen.

"You ever seen one of them before?"

"Party barge," said Jim. He said it in the way you'd normally say "Big ole tour bus comin full of eight-year-olds that like to make fart noises with their armpits."

"I have a feelin about it," I told Jim. "I have a feelin this is it."

"Check," said Jim, and as soon as he said it, he was revvin up the Bass Master, ready to boogie. He settled hisself down into the cockpit, gave the high sign to Yakohira to dump him out the escape hatch, and waited while Yakohira finished watchin the end of *Green Acres* on his Panasonic built-in transistor TV.

After I got finished beatin Yakohira over the head with a bag full of ball bearings, Jim Davis dropped down into the water, fastened his black helmet with his Velcro chinstrap, and busted across the lake at approximately 140 miles an hour, killin numerous endangered species with his monster propeller.

I guess Jim was gone about an hour, but when he got back he had the whole story. He was right about it being a party barge. But it wasn't just any party barge. It had a big banner strung from one end to the other announcing the "Miss Largemouth Bass 1967" beauty pageant, to be held on the second night of the tournament. But on the *first* night, tonight, Miss Largemouth Bass 1966, one Wanda Shanks, would be entertaining all bass competitors in her Miss Largemouth Bass "hospitality barge."

"So what?" I said to Jim. "Sounds like an official tournament event to me."

"You know what it said at the bottom of the banner?"

"Wha'd it say?"

"Sponsored by World Book."

"That slut."

Who was Wanda Shanks? That was what I wanted to know. When you've spent your whole life savings on a plan as deetailed as the one I come up with, you don't like new names poppin up at the last minute. We had a line on the first things we needed to pull off a major felony. We knew exactly *where* José would be, and exactly what time she would be there. Jim and I debated a little bit about whether to make "the snatch" on the first night or the second night, but even I don't have the gall to interrupt anything as sacred as a Miss Largemouth Bass contest, and so it had to be the first night. I started the countdown at 11 hours, 45 minutes, so that we would hit the party barge exactly three hours after the party started. That would give the bassers time to throw back 13, 14 Tequila shooters, which I was countin on to protect me from any insane bass grappler that decided he wanted to defend José's honor or body.

There was only one thing that worried me. Would José be at the party? Who was this Wanda Shanks character that was hostin the deal? What if José was only there for *part* of the time? When you're on a $455,000 Bass Monster, you don't take these things for granted. I sent Jim back out on a "Check out Wanda Shanks" mission, but when he came back an hour later we had nothin. He'd gone into the fishin camp, asked around, tried to find out who she was, stopped in the bait shop and asked leading questions like "Anybody ever slip it to Miss Largemouth?" But so many hands went up we decided people were tryin to turn theirselves in for the publicity. In fact, nobody could remember *having* a Miss Largemouth Bass contest the year before. One guy said he thought we had it confused with the "Drink Like a Fish" contest they had in 1964, but that couldn't be it cause the defending champion and nine other guys had to be buried the next day, so you really couldn't call him *defending* champion, and while we're on the subject, the actual place they were buried was Old Fart's Cove right out where the dam trails off into a shallow place, and the bass just *love* that place. There's always two, three hunnerd pounds caught there ever year.

Anyhow, no Wanda Shanks. But the second piece of news was even worse: The party that night was for the Fellowship of Christian Bass Fishermen from Tupelo, Mississippi, and that meant no Tequila shooters. About all they'd be drinkin is however much Coors they could hide in their trunks. I thought about moving back the attack time, but I didn't wanna confuse Yakohira, who still had trouble tellin the difference between night and day.

No, there was nothin to do but wait. We sat around watchin a little *Mannix* for a while, but I turned it off when Mannix ran into a warehouse wearin a $300 suit and Yakohira kept yellin for the guys named Enzio that were chasin him so they'd shoot Mannix's legs off and then stuff him in the incinerator and put a bullet through Peggy's forehead. This Yakohira was a strange individual.

Since we had a few hours to kill, Jim asked if he could take the Bass Master out and do a little trollin, and I said what the hey and went with him.

Jimbo pulled the Bass Master into a little inlet where the water was real scummy and started flippin a Balsa Big O crankbait plug with a hair leadhead jig and a plastic worm trailer. I don't know if you've ever seen one of these, but if a bass gets a good look at it, he calls for a priest. Sure enough, it wasn't no more than twenty seconds after he pitched that sucker into a mess of muckwater that a big old ugly Papa Bass rammed it through his lips quicker than a punk rocker and it wasn't no more than a couple minutes till we had him floppin around on deck like a Pentecostal.

They have a tradition in these bass tournaments, where you're supposed to flip your bass into the aerated waterwell in your boat so he can go on livin and then, after the weigh-in at the end of the day, you put him back out in the water so somebody else can catch him tomorrow. This makes sense for most people, cause there's no sense in killin a bass for food, since they taste about like a roasted Hush Puppie loafer. But I had a different policy in the Bass Master: I killed em cause I enjoyed watchin em die.

Anyhow, we want on like that for several hours, and I was beginning to see why they called Jim Davis the bass king. We used some weighted slip-sinker plastic worms under a drop-off hump and landed three ten-pounders, then we doodlesocked a Shimmy Gal buckshot floppy worm through a low-hangin branch and flipped in a couple more, then we switched to a banana-head leadhead jig with a pork-rind trailer and a Bagley's Screw Tail so Jim could do his famous double loop cast which can make right angle turns around three trunks and drop into scum ponds up to a half mile away. Course, it was only 67, and we had to use a Zebco 33 reel, so we only got four, five fish this way, and we had to toss two of em back cause the only reason they came in the boat was to meet Jim.

We were out there on the lake for so long that I almost lost track of time, but I looked at my watch and said somethin like, "Jimbo, we got to get back to the roundup point or else Yakohira will think we're dead and start dive-bombin people."

"Yep," Jim said. That's the kind of guy Jim was. He said "Yep" a lot.

I guess it was about sunset when we finally got back on board, strung up the fish, and watched Yakohira do a Benihana demonstration. Unfortunately, it was the first Benihana demonstration he'd ever done, and so we ended up with little pieces of fish all over the floor.

We waited for the cover of nightfall. I checked all the weapons.

"Forward stun gun."

"Yah," said Yakohira.

"Rear stun gun."

"Yah."

"Anti-tank rocket launcher number one."

"Yah."

"Yakohira?"

"Yah."

"Stop sayin 'Yah.' "

"Yah."

Up until this time we'd just been hangin around Smartass Bend, which is a part of Lake Quapaw where some real low cypress branches hang out over the lip of the lake and you can kinda get in there and root around a little bit and be inconspicuous. Course, since the Bass Monster was about 120 feet long, there were limits to how inconspicuous we could be, but one thing we had goin for us was infrared runnin lights, so we could sneak up on the enemy. And the particular enemy we started to sneak up on around nightfall was the Miss Largemouth Bass 1967 Hospitality Barge, which had already started loadin up with Christian Bassers from Mississippi two hours early. Evidently this Wanda Shanks gal was something to see. In fact, Yakohira claimed he knew who she was, said he saw her at a geisha bar in Kyoto in 1955 doing a live-snake act, but then Yakohira also said he saw Bette Davis shot out of a cannon at the Montreal World's Fair.

Like I say, we were on silent runnin. Lights out. Infrared only. All you could hear was this little pooooiiiiiing noise as the sonar bounced off the bottom and hit a bunch of bass and then caromed over into the party barge and back at us so that Yakohira could figure out where we were on his abacus.

"Where are we, Yakohira?"

"Awoooohhh" (flip-flip-whiz-whiz-abacus-abacus) "We in Arkansas."

Anyway, we didn't have to worry about it cause the party barge was lit up like the Astrodome. I told Yakohira to give it 30 degrees to port, and then I regretted tellin him that cause I couldn't remember whether port was left or right and so we ended up turned clear around, but actually that was better cause I needed to dump the Bass Master out of the diaper escape hatch when the time was right.

Next thing I told Yakohira to weigh anchor and he did that, and then I told him to throw the anchor overboard so the boat wouldn't move and he did that, too.

Now it was time to get out the charcoal briquets and put

black all over our faces and jump into our Lloyd Bridges wear and do like a recon mission. But since none of us knew how to scuba dive, we just got into a rubber pontoon boat and paddled our way over to the party barge in disguise. I had this part of it all planned out.

"Whoops!" I said as our black pontoon boat ran smack dab into the back end of their party barge. "Excuse me! That was certainly clumsy!"

A stoned Christian fisherman leaned over the rail and stared at me, or maybe he wasn't stoned. Maybe he was just a Mormon.

"As you can see, we're out here scuba diving for a *National Geographic* special and we seem to have misplaced our depth finder. Do you have a spare?"

The Mormon disappeared without saying anything, and I gave the signal to Jim to start climbin the rope ladder. Good thing I did, too, cause just at that moment I saw the outline of Rhett Beavers moving toward the rail. I knew it was too late to avoid detection, so I made full use of my charcoal face.

Swing looooow, sweet chariotttt . . .

Of course, Jim had no problem at all explaining that he was accompanied by a Negro minstrel scuba diver, and so Rhett didn't suspect a thing. In fact, he leaned over the rail and waved at me.

Of course, at that moment, I wanted to murder the little two-timin goat-roper. But I kept my head.

Joshua fit da battle of Jericho, Jericho, Jericho.

Joshua fit da battle of Jericho, and the walls comeda tumblin down . . .

The two men moved away, out of my sight, and now I knew we were home free. Jim would case the party barge, find out about Wanda Shanks, identify the exact moment that José was expected, and set attack coordinates.

I guess Jim was gone about ten minutes, and then he

came back alone, leaned over the rail, and whispered to me, "We got to stall ten more minutes."

Tote dat barge, lift dat bale, get a little drunk and you land in jaaaaaaiiiil . . . (I hit the low note, too.)

"Ten minutes till Wanda Shanks comes onstage. I want to get a look at her."

I'd walk a million miles for one of your smiles . . .

"They say she's a hot taco."

So I scrunched back down in the pontoon boat and grabbed my scuba britches and rubbed em real hard which you'd understand if you ever had to wear that stuff. And I guess about seven, eight more minutes passed, and then all of a sudden there was this eerie light comin out of the east, like sort of a orange glow, spreadin over the water and makin the fog look like somebody sprayed a giant can of Raid on the lake, and so I looked back over my shoulder, trying to make out what it was and suddenly I saw *the revolvin battle-stations light* circulatin on the Bass Monster.

It was one of those moments where I knew what disaster was about to happen a long time before it did happen. I knew how it happened. I knew why it happened. I knew what stupid things had to go on to make it happen. And it all come down to this:

Nobody told Yakohira that the attack countdown couldn't start as long as me and Jim were *on the party barge.*

From a half mile away, Yakohira fired the first stun-gun tear-gas cannister, and it burst into green flame at the top of its arc and landed directly on the foredeck of the party barge and singed the neckties off three Methodists from Yazoo City. This was the cannister we were gonna use to disable the party while we snatched José, but now *that* was off cause Yakohira fired a second time, and this time 37 orange flares went up from the decks of the Bass Monster and turned the whole western half of Lake Quapaw into a Six Flags Over Texas fireworks show. I jumped up on the deck of the party barge to try to tell everbody to abandon ship before Yakohira blew us out of the water, but just at that exact moment, the Dixieland band began to play the intro for Wanda Shanks and she came sashayin out the other end of the portable indoor Astroturfed glass-bottom fishin area, wearin a four-foot-high ostrich feather on her hair-do and *nothin else on her body* except for a sandwich board that said "WORLD BOOK" in giant letters, only where the O's were supposed to be in "BOOK" there were two nekkid tits instead.

I couldn't believe what I was seeing.

They were José's tits. I'd recognize em anywhere.

Reduced to this.

Tawdry commercialism.

She was too ashamed to put her real name on tits used in such a tasteless manner.

But it was too late to warn José's tits, cause Yakohira had gone looney on us by that time and he hit the button. Originally the anti-personnel grenade-launchers were intended *only* for splashin up the water a little bit and scarin the bejabbers out of the Methodists, but Yakohira trained em directly on the deckhouse and let em fly. Even before the first shells hit there were Christians joinin their bass brethren in the icy depths left and right, bailin this way, bailin that way, the only thing different being the Babtists all thought they were being sent to hell and the Adventists all thought it was the Rapture. I didn't wait to see whose hiney was gonna hang, I ran straight for José, made a flying spread-eagle tackle to push her out of the line of fire, and was immediately knocked unconscious cause I forgot she was wearin a sandwich board at the time. The next thing I knew I was flounderin around in the water, covered up with life preservers and whinin

Presbyterians, tryin to make my way back to the pontoon boat. Jim Davis was way ahead of me, though. He'd already free-styled it back to the Bass Monster, crept up through the escape hatch, disarmed Yakohira, who was wearing three ammo belts across his chest and holdin an Uzi submachine gun in each hand, and moved the Bass Monster into position to start pickin up survivors. Of course, the Miss Largemouth Bass hospitality barge was in flames by that time, and there wasn't much we could do except watch her sink and hope there wasn't any Buddhists on there meditatin.

And then I saw somethin that I'll never forget as long as I live. Floating out in the middle of the lake, you could just barely see it by the light of the flares that were still burnin, was the "World B K" sandwich board, and of course it did say "World B K" on it because José's tits were nowhere to be found. I swam over to it anyhow, hoisted it up into the pontoon boat, but somewhere her cold, freezing, braless body was abandoned to the horrors of Lake Quapaw.

I sat in my black pontoon boat, shiverin, while the cinders died out on the water, a broken man, chastened, changed, lost. I sat there through the whole night long, singing Negro spirituals.

In the morning I found a memento of José, soggy and weather-beaten, clinging to a spar, floating near my pontoon boat. I reached out into the water and grabbed it, clutched it to my chest. It was the "R" volume, waterlogged but still readable. Raamses to Ryukyu Islands. And I knew that, whatever else happened, I would always have "R."

13

My Battle with Cancer

After I lost José I had no more desire to live. Fortunately, the Arkansas State Police had no more desire for me to live, either, and so they slapped my hiney in the Saline County Jail on some kinda charges of "mass terrorism" or "nukin a bass tournament" or something like that, I can't remember, and for a few weeks there, while it was in the newspapers ever day, I thought it was probly "Go direct to Death Row, Electric Chair City," the whole nine yards, but then they figured out about all they could pin on me was destruction of a commercial party barge for sinister purposes. But my lawyer, Bubba Barclay, drove up to bail me out, and he convinced em that I was a man under the influence of insane jealous passions, and also that Yakohira was one man, acting alone. I won't go into all the petty politics of the situation, about how the bass tournament had to return all the entry fees and everthing, but the bottom line is Jim and me walked. Jim was p.o.ed, World Book was p.o.ed, everbody said I owed em nineteen hunnerd jillion dollars for damages, and so I settled out of court by agreeing to pay em everthing I owned. Of course, all I owned at the time was a Bass Monster. They took it, too, my pride and joy. It was almost as bad as losin José. Then they let me out, with five bucks, the clothes on my back, and the Merc. The first thing I did, I drove the

Merc to a K mart and used the five bucks for clothes for the rest of my body besides my back.

It took me most of 1967 to figure out there was more meaning to my life than chasin José's titties. I realize a lot of you are cheering at this point, because you're under the false impression that I'm finished making titty jokes and I'm gonna stop beating that dead horse. One thing I've noticed is that very immature, brain-damaged adolescent minds often have a fixation on female breasts. But let's face it, that's the kind of fifties humor that we don't need anymore, specially in the eighties, when we're so *blasé* about tits. But that's not something that happened over-night. We had to go through the sixties to get there— Haight-Ashbury, LSD, Arlo Guthrie, and a lot of really bad movies. I know. I was there. I lived through the six-ties. Actually, I lived through the year 1967. I missed the rest of the sixties. But '67 was the biggie. That was the year I lost José, the year I lost my titty bar, the year I got arrested for armed invasion of a party barge, and the year I spun out on U.S. 59 South and flipped the Merc into a stock pond. The stock pond wouldn't of been so bad, if there hadn't been three Polled Herefords takin a bath in there at the time. Two of em died instantly, and the third one was in critical condition for four days before Stovall's Cripple-Cow Service come by to pick him up. Vern Stovall was a friend of mine, or else there could of been a nasty scandal. I swear I was sober and I never saw any of the alleged Herefords before that night, but you know how these things get twisted whenever beef cattle are involved. I didn't want another Chappaquiddick. Speak-ing of twisted, the Merc got fried as soon as those rear speakers hit the water. I'm surprised I excaped with only minor clothing loss.

Pretty soon I realized I didn't have a car or a titty to my name. So I did what anybody would do in a case like that. I

went to Mexico. Mexico's always been the place you go
when you wanna disappear. First they take your money.
Then they take all your stereo equipment. Then they
make you disappear.

The actual place I decided to disappear in was Matamoros, Mexico, cause I always heard you could get Laetrile
treatments down there even if you didn't have cancer. I
figured if I started in on em now, I could keep smokin
another forty, fifty years before I started wheezin like the
accordion player at the American Legion hall. This was
just a theory I had, but I finally found me a qualified
Meskin physician, Farturo Robledo "El Doctoro," and he
confirmed that I could prevent cancer for a measly 22
pesos a week as long as I didn't start eatin those goat-
burgers they serve up over by the El Mercado. So the way
I looked at it, first day in Mexico and I was already one up
on life by startin cancer treatments.

Matamoros is one of the most beautiful Meskin border
towns in the greater Matamoros area. Sometimes you can
stand in the middle of Matamoros on a hot summer night,
close your eyes, and when you open em up again, everything you own will be gone. At other times you can take
deep breaths and just *smell* the place and it takes you back
in time, this sense of nostalgia sweeps over you, and you
can't quite remember where you've smelled it before, it
smells so familiar and so comforting, so close, so encom-
passing, and then it hits you—it smells just like your mother's womb.

Hence the name. Matamoros. "The Mother City." Or, if
you want a more literal translation of exactly what they
call it in Mexico, Matamoros is "Place of the Bull Dropping." In fact, on Sunday afternoons, you can go down to
the main square of the city, the Plaza de Taco Bueno, and
listen to the El Padre from the cathedral recite the ancient legend of how the town came to be, beginning in the

year when the giant Lizard-skin Shoe Salesman swooped into northern Mexico with a 4,000-pound sample case, scattering the residents across the desert and imprisoning the virgins in patent-leather Size 4's. For forty years the people groaned and wailed and begged for sweat socks. But the town was liberated when a giant Snake named Art bought up all the empty property, foreclosed on the people that ran away, and built a roller disco that sucked in all the tourist money. Then, when the giant Lizard-skin Shoe Salesman came back, Art the Snake lured him into an abandoned stucco bolo-tie store and, as soon as he walked through the door—*wham!*—dropped a bull on him. Nobody knows how he did it. Nobody knows how he got the bull into the building, how he suspended the bull in mid-air, how he got the bull's cooperation, or why he would use a bull to kill somebody. But it had to be mysterious and symbolic or else the people wouldn't of come back home and worshipped Art the Snake and built the town. Funny thing about the story, though, the bull didn't kill the giant Lizard-skin Shoe Salesman—just paralyzed him from the ankles down. But it ruined his reputation. He had to go rent a booth at the bus station and sell velvet lizard paintings the rest of his life.

Hence the name "Place of the Bull Dropping," or, if you speak more classical Spanish, "El Toro Caca Grande."

I'll never forget the day I walked into Matamoros the first time. I didn't have papers or a passport, so I had to pay this guy Esteban to smuggle me across the Rio Grande. There was six of us starting a new life that night— me, four Jewish guys from Brooklyn, and a lounge singer named Vinnie Grunge. Vinnie had a single out at the time you may of heard of, called "Mama Mia, Set Me Free-a," and his agent told him to go wait out the reviews in Mexico. What a guy. Vinnie loved his work so much he wore a pale purple tuxedo shirt with chest ruffles at all times, and

if he said it to me once, he said it a hunnerd times, "Joey
Bobby"—that's what he called me— "Joey Bobby, there's-
a no business like-a tow business." Vinnie lived by that
philosophy. Vinnie always wanted to go into his brother's
towing business in Queens, but it didn't work out and he
had to go on the road. But he loved the tow business
anyhow.

So the six of us all paid this guy Esteban five bucks to
smuggle us over to Matamoros and we all met up together
outside Brownsville one night at midnight and we said a
prayer to Jehovah. The reason we picked Him instead of
God the Babtist is we had four Jews, one Catholic, and me,
and I figured, what the heck, if God chose em, he don't
care if they talk funny. The only guy I worried about was
Vinnie, cause whenever he got into trouble he had this
habit of grabbing hold of the crucifix around his neck and
singing old Andy Williams medleys to it. But I calmed
Vinnie down and threw some zebra skins over his tuxedo
shirt to cut down the glare and pretty soon we were ready
to go. Esteban gave us some last-minute instructions.

"Whatever hoppen," he said, "do not spicka Inglace."

"So what are we supposed to spicka?" I asked him.

"Spicka Fronsace."

"And how does that go?"

"Repayta after may. 'Voolay voo.'"

"Voolay voo."

"Muy bien. Now 'Voolay voo Marlboros.'"

"Voolay voo Marlboros."

"Repayta."

"Voolay voo Marlboros."

"That's what you say evrabody."

"Voolay voo Marlboros?"

"Muy bien."

So here we were, ready to leave our native country and
start a new life in the wonderland across the river, and I

have to say, we were scared. I only had enough supplies for one day—12 cans of cold Raviolios and a canteen full of Mountain Dew. It wasn't much, but it would have to do. I stuffed the Raviolios down my pants so they wouldn't clank together during the actual crossing, and I have the scars to prove it. Vinnie helped out by hiding some Fritos under his tuxedo shirt, but when we got to the other side it was not a pretty sight. Finally, we were ready to go.

"Five cents pliz," said Esteban.

"More money?" I said.

"Nid five cents for toll."

So we all fished down in our backpacks and came up with nickels and forked em over to Esteban, and then he motioned for us to quietly follow him. We only stopped once—to check out of our hotel. Then we were off to Mexico. Esteban led us down the main street of Browns-ville to the International Bridge and motioned for us to follow him to the first toll booth. When we got there, he put all the nickels in the turnstile and we passed through it one at a time. Several people stared at us as we made our break, acting like they'd never seen Jewish guys in full military combat fatigues before, but we ignored em and sprinted across the bridge. When we got to the other side, there were about twenty Meskin guys in official uniforms waiting on us. They said something to us in Spanish, and all we had to say was "Voolay voo Marlboros?"

As soon as we said that, they waved us on through. We were *free*. We made it. I can't really describe the feeling. One day we were in the United States. The next day— Mehico. It was so *easy*. We still couldn't quite believe it. Everthing was set up just like Esteban said it would be. *Twenty soldiers waiting to make sure we got across okay.* What a country this was. Suddenly we all had new homes.

I guess the first friend I made in Mexico, besides Vinnie of course, was Farturo Robledo "El Doctoro," who's been my personal cancer doctor and chief financial advisor ever since then. Farturo had a little place down on Cancer Row when I first met him. It wasn't much—just a few cardboard boxes pasted together, really—but it was enough to get him started. Farturo was fresh out of Universidad, which is where he went to study Mexican drug consumption and modern tourism. He was a straight-A student, and his thesis was called "Influence of *TV Guide* Advertising on Mexican Weight-Loss Camps, 1955–1960." Farturo, you probly figured out by now, was one smart Meskin.

I'll never forget the first thing Farturo ever said to me. "Joe Bob," he said, "you don't have cancer."

He recognized that fact, right there on the spot, just by studying my astrology chart. That's the kinda guy he was.

I said, "I know I don't, Farturo, but I wanna hire you anyway. Is there any law that says you got to have cancer to get cancer treatments?"

"No way, José."

"Then sign me up."

Farturo, by the way, was the man who invented the term "No way, José." I know a lot of people *claim* they invented it, but I wanna set the record straight right now and give credit where credit's due. In fact, Farturo also invented the term "Sell the Alamo!" Farturo has that kind of mind. He taught me everthing I know about the binness world.

That was a quiet time for me, a peaceful time. I remember the long, drowsy afternoons, when Farturo and I would take *siesta* with the patients, lounging under the palms, drinking Coco-Locos, waxing our *serapes*. Sometimes the little *mestizo* children would frolic nekkid in the public fountain on the square, and we'd have to call the cops and have em arrested. The wind would rustle the giant palm leaves and whistle old Yugoslavian folk ballads.

And ever once in a while Farturo would get up from his hammock and change his shirt.

Mexico does something to you. It seeps into your brain and creeps into your body and gradually takes you over, and finally you wake up one day and find out you're a Meskin yourself and you know what? You don't wanna change your shirt anymore.

I don't remember exactly when it happened to me. I guess I'd been there four, five months, and I was into pretty advanced cancer treatments. I was taking Laetrile, essence-of-prune, Vita-Mex, and Tequila shooters three times daily. Then I went down to The Clinic one day, started to get into my cardboard box, and at the last minute I stopped and said, "Farturo?"

Farturo was down the street at the time, delivering a weasel, so I had to wait a couple hours before he came back and I could say it again. "Farturo?"

"*Sí, José Roberto.*"

"Farturo, I think I'm cured."

Farturo folded his arms across his enormous belly and looked me up and down, calculating my hemoglobin.

"You come to me, you *always* be cured."

"No, I think I'm cured of José. I think I'm over her now. You know that dream I kept having?"

"The one where José explodes her tits at a nuclear test site in Los Alamos?"

"No, the one where José conducts the Boston Pops with her tits."

"The one where she does the John Philip Sousa marches or the title theme from *Oklahoma*?"

"John Philip Sousa marches."

"Sí, I know that one."

"Well, last night I started to have that dream, and it got to the piccolo solo and all of sudden José fell off the podium."

"Fell off the podium?"

"Disappeared plumb out of sight."

"You never told me there was a podium."

"The podium don't matter. She fell off it."

"If I knew about the podium, I would have sent you to another psychiatric specialist," said Farturo.

"What's the big deal about the podium?"

"Was she *standing* on the podium or sitting?"

"She was conducting the goldurn Boston Pops. What do you *think* she was doing? Of *course* she was standing."

"Oh no."

"What?"

"This ees not good."

"What?"

"Was she carrying anything?"

"Just a baton."

"A baton! A baton?? Why didn't you tell me she was carrying a baton?"

"It didn't seem important."

And I guess it was right after that we started my treatments all over again. It was obvious to Farturo that José was down there inside me somewhere, rootin around in my psychology, workin me over like a midget wrestler. There was nothing I could do about it. Farturo told me I might have to be in Mexican analysis for years. During the worst of it, I had to be on the couch two hours ever afternoon after *siesta*. We would lay there in our adjoining hammocks and Farturo would do word associations.

"Just say the first word that comes into your head," he'd tell me.

"Okay."

Then he'd wait a minute till I relaxed.

"Mother," he'd say.

"Mother," I'd say.

"Wife."

"Wife."
"Hot."
"Hot."
"José."
"José."
"Food."
"Food."
"Inna Gadda Divida."
"Inna Gadda Divida."

Sometimes we'd go on like this for thirty, forty minutes, and I always noticed, as long as we did it, that the first word that popped into my head was always the same word Farturo said to me. It's an interesting psychological fact about me that's not true of most people. That's why I had to stay in analysis so long.

Course, even though Farturo changed my life forever, he wasn't my only Meskin friend. There was Juan and Pablo and little Ricardo and Uncle Poncho and, of course, Wolfgang. Wolfgang—boy, was he a strange one! Always sneakin around the clinic, tellin everybody he was from "south Mexico." And once a week he'd go down to the bank and cash all this German money and act like he just happened to get it "by accident" when he went shopping over in Brownsville. Twenty years Wolfgang was doing this. Finally one day I said to him, "Hey! Wolfie Baby! What's with the Doitchie Dollars?" And I won't say that Wolfgang was *irritated* by the remark. He just suggested a few toxic combustible chemicals he could pour down my pants the next time he saw me.

Anyhow, I bring up Wolfgang because he was a frontal lobotomy expert, and you may recall, around '67 or '68, it was very hard to get frontal lobotomies in this country. Sometimes you had to get on a waiting list. People could wait seven, eight years just to get the first ice-pick treatment. And so Wolfgang was an intersting guy to me, cause

I was considering a lobotomy myself, due to my problem with word associations.

The doctors tried to talk me out of it. "What if it doesn't take?" said Farturo. "You know, sometimes they work. Sometimes they don't. You might wake up and be a South African tribal chief. Maybe the surgeon slips *just a little bit* and what happens? You wind up selling room deodorizers at 7-Eleven."

"Do they carry those?"

"And who knows? You could wake up and find out you're a liberal."

That was enough for me. No frontal lobotomies until they perfect the technique. So I did the next best thing. I went into Intensive Super-Deluxe Pyramid-Sweepstakes Analysis, the kind where you go out in the desert with eight or nine people, strip nekkid, "encounter" each other, and start screaming like jackals undergoing electrolysis. I had some permanent skin loss as a result of this treatment, but it resulted in definite dividends, like the knowledge that I'm a Schizoid Degenerate. That's the official psychiatric term for it. You wouldn't think learning something like that could change your life, since there's probly ten or fifteen other Schizoid Degenerates in the world, but I don't know. Once I *knew* this about myself, I didn't have to worry anymore about being "different." It was an incredible freedom. For the first time in my life, I could act like a complete idiot without the *shame.*

You know, it kind of makes you wonder, how many other people are there in the world who are truly Schizoid Degenerates in their hearts but just don't know it yet? They don't have access to a really good analysis program. Or maybe they know it, but they're afraid to tell anybody. They think they're the only one in the world. That's why, from the day of that discovery until this day, I've always devoted at least one day a month to counseling sessions with impressionable young children who don't know enough about life yet to make that big psychiatric decision. They're going along, playing Little League baseball, getting A's on their report cards, riding bicycles and catching bullfrogs, and they can't figure out what's wrong with their life. Some of these pathetic little kids don't even know *anything* is wrong with their life. That's where I come in. I convince these kids that they *can* be Schizoid Degenerates, if they really want to, and they can do it today, right now, without waiting until they grow up and it costs em $9,000 a year in professional psychiatric advice. I can't tell you how many lives I've saved with this simple program, the "Big Pervert" brotherhood. I don't want these kids to have to go through what I went through—lookin at all those nekkid Meskins in the desert. There's an easier way.

14

The Black Market

It was pretty plain to me that I couldn't hang around Farturo's clinic forever, no matter how much the cardboard-box life might appeal to us all. It was time for me to get a job. Problem was, you can't get a job in Mexico unless you have a hundred dollars or else a Brown Card, and really it's better to have a hundred dollars cause it cost about three hundred dollars to get somebody to write you out a Brown Card. But since I didn't have a hundred dollars *or* a Brown Card, I went to Farturo and said, "Farturo, I know you can't keep giving me free cancer cures forever. I need to get a job so someday I can pay you what I owe you."

And Farturo kinda liked the sound of that idea and so he fixed me up a job running over to Brownsville three, four times a day to pick up Nehru Jackets at Bandolero Mall. You see, at the time there was an embargo on Nehru exports to Mexico due to the fact that a lot of *irresponsible* members of the Meskin Commonist Party were running the Nehru Jackets down to Havana, scissoring off the labels, and using em as uniforms for the Cuban Navy. So sometimes if you had an unscissored Nehru, you could bring ten, fifteen bucks for it in Matamoros. That may not sound like a lot of money *today*, but back in '67 it was ten, fifteen bucks.

So anyhow, I'd head over to Bandolero Mall, buy a Nehru, and *wear* it back across the International Bridge. As long as they thought all the Nehrus were for my personal use, we were fine. But all this runnin back and forth between Mexico and Bandolero Mall finally started getting to me, and fortunately that's right at the time when I got the best dang binness idea of my entire life.

Here's what I was noticing. Ever day I crossed from Mexico into the U.S., and ever day I had to wait in line while the Border Patrol and the Immigration guys turned these Meskins upside down, trying to shake some weed out of their pockets, and then took a Roto-Rooter crew and went through their cars like buzzards at a prairie-dog convention, and then made em show enough papers to print the Guadalajara phone book, and then finally they'd turn most of em back anyhow cause they'd be on expired visas or they'd be in trouble for sneakin in last year or some other crapola they'd make up on the spot.

But then right after that some guy would come through in a Chevy Caprice, and his car would be full of bullfighter paintings and sombreros and dozing-Meskin bookends and pinatas—and the guy with the Border Patrol, he'd just look in there and *wave him on through!*

Ever day I went across the border, and ever day the same deal happened. One day I saw this '53 Rambler with 37 Meskins riding it, and even though it looked like they were all members of the same fambly, the Border Patrol stopped em and asked em all for papers and sent 20, 25 of em back. The next guy walks up carryin a paper-mache rooster—*no problema.*

So by this time I decided I wanted to do something for the Meskin people. I guess it took about a month to get all the arrangements made, take out a loan from Farturo (I had to cut him in for 20 per cent), and put out my sign as Matamoros's first "Immigration Consultant."

First day on the job, I went and took up my position—
halfway across the bridge, smack dab on the U.S.-Mexico
line—and I waited for some action. Sure enough, I'm looking off to the west, watching the gurgling Rio Grande
gurgle, and here come about 15 Meskins about a mile
upriver, dartin through the water carrying mattresses on
their backs, trying to get to the other side before the cops
notice they look like the Polish Olympic rafting team.
And sure enough, one of the Border Patrol dogs sniffs em
out, scares the bejabbers out of em, and pretty soon we
got some old boy in a metal hat takin down their names
and loadin em onto a school bus for the ride back to
Matamoros.

This time, though, soon as that bus got to the Meskin
side of the border, I was there waitin on it. And while they
were comin down the steps, I kept saying, "Who the
heck's in charge here?"

And ever time I said that, they'd say, *"No comprendo,
Senor."*

And so I saw that wasn't workin and I said, "Who'll
gimme three bucks to get to the Newnited States?"

And all of a sudden about ten of em comprendoed. So I
rounded em all up together and I picked out the one that
looked the most intelligent, a guy named Felipe, and I
said, "Okay, listen up here, Phil, and I want you to trans-
late this for all the other *amigos,* is that understood?"

Phil picked a few cockleburrs off his teeth and nodded
in agreement.

"You guys look like *crap."* (I decided to start off with my
strongest stuff.)

"Look at yourselves," I said. "You been muckin around
in the river, you got alligator gar bites all over your shins,
you got so much mud on your shirts that you can scrub em
all day long and you won't make that turquoise parakeet
stitching show up ever again."

I could see em starting to look at each other knowingly, as though to say "What parakeet stitching?"

"You've been humiliated by the Newnited States Government."

I was startin to get their attention now.

"And you *lost* your mattresses, didn't you?"

As fate would have it, just as I said that, a battered mattress came floating down the river, crashing against the bridge spars, breaking up into Beautyrest flotsam.

"You guys are pretty pitiful illegal aliens, aren't you?"

At this point there were scattered shouts of *"Arriba!"* I have no idea what this means.

"You guys don't even deserve the *name* illegal aliens."

"Yeah!" one of em said.

"You ain't illegal . . ."

"Yeah!"

"And you *sure* ain't aliens."

"Tell us some more!"

"So I wonder what you are if you're not illegal aliens?"

"What are we?"

"You must be legal . . ."

"Yeah!"

"And you must be human."

"Yeah!"

"Legal humans is all you are."

"That's right."

"And what you *wanna* be is illegal aliens."

"You said it."

"Wouldn't that be nice?"

"Sí, sí, Senor!"

"But we can't do it standin around here, now can we?"

"No! No!"

"Okay, then, let's follow me."

So I led em all down to El Mercado, where I had me a shop sub-leased out from Consuelo Martini, the kingpin of the Matamoros tourist industry. You probly heard of him. Consuelo *owned* tourism in that town. He wore velvet lapels *in the daytime.* You heard of the Meskin jumping bean? Consuelo invented it. Meskin hat dance? Held the exclusive northeast Mexico franchise on it. Ever see one of the billfolds with a cactus on it? Just *try* to make one of those without forking over a commission to Consuelo Martini. The man was, as we say in Mehico, *grandy.* In fact, they called him "Mister Wanna-Buy-a-Watch." Or, to use the Spanish, "El Supremo Clockadero."

Consuelo gave me a prime location on aisle 8-A of El Mercado, right between "T-Shirt Fiesta" on my right and "Chess Sets Unlimited, Specializing in Weird Rock Formations You Can Give As Gifts to People That Never Play Chess" on my left.

My sign was simple:

Senor José Roberto
Immigracion y Camisas Nehru

As you entered the store, to your left was a nine-foot-high rack of dozing-Meskin bookends, hand carved out of plastic. To your right was a couple rows of rock burros, a few straw sombreros with "Viva!" on the hatband, and my special line of fat-lady designer fiesta dresses, also known as cattle blankets. At the back, behind the official immigration consulting counter, you had your velvet bullfighter, your velvet Aztec calendar, and your "Buenos Dias" wall plaque to hang up over the stove and practice your Spanish with.

So on the day I'm talkin about, all ten guys crowded into the store and waited with bad breath.

I walked over and grabbed a dozing-Meskin bookend off the shelf.

"What do you think I'm holding here in my hand?"

Several hands went up.

"A bookend?"

"A doorstop?"

"A weapon?"

"Well," I said, chuckling to myself, "you're all right—and you're all *wrong.*"

Again there were scattered shouts of *"Arriba!"* adding to the confusion in the room.

"This dozing-Meskin bookend is your ticket to the Newnited States."

There were scattered shouts of "Huh?"

"All you need in order to travel freely between Mexico and La America is this little jewel right here. Lemme tell you what'll happen if you get one of these. Pack up your stuff, put on your best clothes, even get in the car if you have one. Go over to the International Bridge *carrying your dozing-Meskin bookend in a highly visible place on your person,* and calmly go through the customs line on the other side of El River. You know what will happen then?"

"He make us eempty our pockets, tear up our car, laugh at the leetle ones, and send us back to Mehico."

"Heh heh heh," I said. Do you realize how hard it is to say that? But that's what I said, at that moment, and I've never been able to say it again the rest of my life. I practice all the time at home, but I can never get it right—can't make the "h" at the end of the "heh" come out right. But that's beside the point.

"Heh heh heh," I said, "that's where you're *wrong wrong wrong wrong and wrong.*"

There were scattered pockets of silence.

"What will happen," I said, "is the Border Patrol officer will take one look at that dozing-Meskin bookend and he'll *wave you through!*"

There were scattered shouts of "What a jerk!"

"No, no," I said, "you don't have to take *my* word for it. Go down to the bridge. Stand there and watch. Watch em all day. Just *wait* till somebody walks across that bridge carryin a dozing-Meskin bookend, and you'll see what I mean. No searches, no questions, *no problema.* And do you know why?"

"*¿Qué?*" they all said in unison.

"Because it's a secret that only *Americans* know. *I'm* an American. *I* know it. The Border Patrol knows it. Now I've told *you* about it. The dozing-Meskin bookend is the universal symbol of international peace, or maybe it's the international symbol of the Kiwanis Club. I don't really remember. I'm not up on my American history. But anyway, all you guys need to know is, *anybody* carrying a dozing-Meskin bookend is welcome in our country. And do you wanna know the best part?"

"*Sí, sí, Senor!*"

"This is where you get em, and they *only* cost sixty pesos."

They stood there without saying anything, and for a minute I thought I was gonna lose em. I thought they might figure out that a dozing-Meskin bookend is not the *only* thing you could get waved through with, and so maybe they'd go next door and get some el cheapo rock chess sets, which don't have near the workmanship my hand-carved plastic dozing Meskins have.

Finally, this one little guy in the back piped up and said, "What if it don't work?"

I looked at the guy with an expression of total panic and calmly replied, "What do you *mean*, if it don't work? Didn't I just *tell* you how it works?"

He didn't say a word.

"Okay, that's it," I said. "You guys get outta here. You wanna go to America and start a new life as official illegal aliens—sixty pesos. Wanna stand around here lookin like legal humans? Forget it. I got better things to do with my time. I'll go find some guys that *really* wanna be illegal. I'll comb the streets, I'll brush the sewers, I'll shampoo the gutters. I'll . . ."

"Okay."

I almost didn't hear him, he said it so quiet.

"What was that?"

"Okay," the little guy said, and he reached down in his pocket and dug out sixty pesos and slammed em down on the counter. Then he grabbed the dozing-Meskin bookend out of my hand, turned, and walked out of the store. It all happened so fast I didn't even have time to thank him. And then, in a flash, the place was empty. All the rest of the guys had followed him out into the street, forming a caravan of would-be illegal aliens on their way to the International Bridge, to check out the merchandise. I started getting a little nervous about the *implications* of this thing, so I went ahead and locked up the store and followed em on out.

We started out through the streets of downtown Matamoros, just the eleven of us, not saying a word, marching along behind the grim little guy with the bookend clenched in his fist. Then, as we passed the doorway of Pepe's Off-Track Betting and Pizzeria, a couple of little kids noticed us and started running along behind us. Next thing I knew Pepe himself came out, rubbing his hands on his apron to get rid of the newsprint, and he yelled out, *"¿Qué pasa?"*

"Federico is going to America!"

So anyhow, it just happened that whoever yelled that back at Pepe was real close to Federico's house, and Federico's wife heard it and she stuck her head out the window and noticed the mob marching down the street and then started freaking out when she saw Federico at the head of the line. She didn't care if he went to America, but she'd seen him off that morning with a perfectly good mattress on his back and now he evidently didn't have it anymore and she thought maybe he'd traded in his mattress for some Guatemalan whiskey and so she ran out into the street chattering some Meskin-wife stuff at him.

Well, one thing led to another and pretty soon we had sixty, seventy people following along behind us, wondering what was going on and why Federico was marching toward the river with a dozing-Meskin bookend in his fist. Some of em tried to find out by yelling, "Hey! Federico! Got a door that won't stay open?" Or, "So, Federico, I see you're on your way to kill somebody. Mind if I ask who it is?"

But nothin seemed to work. Federico just kept marching towards the American border, and I have to admit, it was about this point when I seriously considered making a run for it, cause I started wondering what would happen if the Border Patrol grabbed Federico and broke his face in with that dozing-Meskin bookend. But my conscience got the better of me, and I decided to do the honorable thing, and not to run away like a slimy reptile until the last possible moment.

There was probly about two hunnerd of us by the time we got to the bridge, but Federico didn't even stop, he just pushed on through the Meskin Army and started across the Rio and by now he had such an iron grip on that bookend I was starting to worry he might bust the custom plastic sombrero into 9,000 pieces, but fortunately it was a *reinforced* childproof custom plastic sombrero and so it held up like a champion. I guess we all got about halfway across the bridge, right to the place where they have the big trash barrels that say "Dump your drugs here and we won't stuff a club down your throat," and then gradually the crowd stopped moving—probly too afraid to go any closer, thinking they might be identified with Federico when the cops started doing surgery on his *cabesa*. So there we were, all bunched up on the bridge, blocking traffic both directions, just standing there like Brangus cattle, starin down at Federico as he kept marching towards Brownsville, holding that dozing-Meskin bookend like a loaded pistol.

"Don't do it, Federico!"

I had to knock the guy out that said that. It wasn't something I *wanted* to do. It didn't make me *happy* to do it. But part of the idea is you don't make a Big Deal out of walkin across the Newnited States border with a dozing-Meskin bookend.

It was too late anyway, though, cause about that time everbody up on the bridge started yelling at Federico, whistling, screaming, saying stuff like, "Send me some Dallas Cowboys sweatshirts!" And there was nothing I could do about it. Here we were, trying to get this guy safely into the U.S., and we had three mariachi bands and seventeen bullfight announcers standing around yelling grocery orders at him. I decided there was nothing else to do—I just stood there with my Meskin Fiesta Shirt gettin drenched with sweat, bunching up around the half-moons in my armpits.

Next thing I notice, there's Mad Dog Wallace standin in one of the booths on the other side, and, course, you probly heard of Mad Dog, he's the guy that's strip-searched ever guy that's tried to cross that bridge since 1948. Mad Dog's been in the Border Patrol since 1912, and he believes they're too lenient—anybody that leaves the Newnited States, even if they're American, ought not to ever be allowed back in, just on principle. So Mad Dog, he's over there in the booth, stacking up the citations he's wrote up in the last thirty minutes, and here I see Federico *heading directly for Mad Dog's booth.*

You can probly imagine what I did at this point.

Then again, maybe you can't. Cause what I did was, I went over the side. I looked down at the water and the rocks and the empty Dr Pepper cans and the mattress stuffings, and it looked a whole heck of a lot better than anything that was about to come down up on the bridge, and so I did a Guatemalan Duck Dive off the bridge, lost all consciousness as soon as I hit the water, and don't remember anything else till I woke up three days later on Boca Chica Beach.

The rest of this story I got to piece together from eye-witness accounts, since I wasn't there to see it my ownself. I should warn you that the rest of this chapter will be the only part of Western Civilization that I han't personally witnessed, but I felt it my duty to bring you the *entire* history of the world and not just the parts that *I* think are important.

Okay. So. Best as I can tell, as soon as I made the jump, three things happened all at once:

Numero Uno: About half the people standing up on the bridge saw me go over the side, rushed over to the railing, and watched me get swallowed up in an Eddy and spit out in a Shirley and tossed over on my backside and thrown up in the air like Flipper and pretty much turned into a piece of scenery for future episodes of Jacques Cousteau.

Numero Two-o: The other half of the people had their eyes riveted on Federico, and they started chanting ancient Aztec snake rituals to help him get to the other side.

Numero Three-o: Mad Dog Wallace heard all the commotion, saw me go over the side, looked up and noticed the unruly mob making the bridge sway back and forth, and immediately picked up the phone and called for "emergency back-up units to assist with probably Communist-inspired political demonstration."

Suddenly, Federico was standing right in front of Mad Dog, holding his dozing-Meskin bookend, searching Mad

Dog's face for some sign. But Mad Dog kept staring up at the crowd on the bridge.

"Senor?" said Federico.

Mad Dog picked up the phone again, dialed the riot squad, and started loading his 25-millimeter semi-automatic government-issue assault carbine.

"Senor!" said Federico, thrusting the dozing-Meskin bookend at Mad Dog.

When Mad Dog continued to ignore him, Federico held the bookend in *both hands,* raised it over his head, and started jumping up and down in an attempt to get Mad Dog to look directly at it.

"Senor Mad Dog!"

At the sound of his name, Mad Dog turned and looked at the little guy with the bookend.

"Oh," he said.

Mad Dog gave an almost invisible *flick* of his left hand.

Federico wasn't sure what that meant.

Mad Dog then gave a slow *wave* of his left hand, the signal that Federico could go on through the check-station, unmolested, free, now an *official* illegal alien.

As soon as Mad Dog gave the second wave, the crowd on the bridge erupted in cheers and ovations, and a 24-hour celebration began. By the time the riot squad arrived, everbody had already run back down the other side of the bridge, popped open all the Nicaraguan champagne they could find, and started performing the El Chico on their heads. People in Matamoros *still* talk about the party they had that night.

Course, I wasn't there to see it. Like I say, I didn't come to till three days later, and that was only due to a wino kickin me in the groin until I had to get up and permanently maim him. Even after he rousted me out, I wasn't too keen on goin back to Matamoros, cause I figured by now Consuelo Martini voided my lease for violating the

Meskin Tourism Ethical Code and it would probly take a couple hunnerd bucks to get my ethics reinstated. I didn't have any choice, though. I had to go back. I couldn't run out on Farturo like that. After all, he was the man who cured me of cancer.

I guess you can imagine how surprised I was, then, when I got back to Matamoros, went over to the El Mercado, and there was a line around the block three times, people waiting to get in so they could buy dozing-Meskin bookends and start a new life in America. Course, I was even more surprised when I got up close and saw the store was *open* and somebody was in there selling off my merchandise. I took off running as soon as I saw what was happening, but the closer I got to the store, the weirder things got. People waiting in line started recognizing me, and soon as they did they took off their hats, crossed themselves, fell flat on their faces on the street, and started praising "San José Roberto" like flashers at a nudist convention. I had to stop and bless twelve of em just so they'd let me by.

When I finally got a few feet from the door of my place, I heard an unmistakable voice coming from inside:

"I can knock four pesos off the medallion, but only if you take double burro paperweights."

I stopped stock-still as a bird dog.

"Pinata discounts with a two-hundred-peso billfold purchase."

It was a voice so familiar—and yet it couldn't be. It was impossible. It was a cruel joke of nature. It was a bad sitcom plot. It was God playing Parcheesi. It was herpes on a walrus. It was . . .

Oh my God, it was HIM.

I was so confused and terrified that I almost broke down the front door, which was impossible cause I didn't have a front door.

"Rhett!"

And sure enough, there was Rhett Beavers, holding court at the back of the store. *He was alive! And if Rhett was alive, that meant I still had one more chance to kill him.*

He had a La-Z-Boy recliner set up behind the "immigration consultant" desk, and he was swatting flies while he gave out illegal-alien advice. I stood watching him with my mouth hangin open like an amphibious troop carrier.

"Excuse me, just a minute, Joe Bob," he said as everyone in the store knelt reverently before me and said thanks to God in Latin. "Mr. Gonzales, if you intend to take thirty-seven members of your immediate family to America with you, then you are *definitely* gonna need some straw roosters, six or seven of them serapes, three Nehru jackets—"

"Three Nehru jackets?" said Gonzales.

"Okay, okay," said Rhett, "we won't make your wife wear one. Two Nehru jackets, Acapulco Meskin-on-a-seesaw snow scene, four sombreros . . ."

And Rhett kept at it like this for another five, ten minutes until he finally took 240 pesos off the guy and then sold him a hand-truck to carry all his immigration merchandise out of the store with, and then Rhett said, "How the heck you doing, Joe Bob? Preciate you puttin me in your settlement. This beats all heck out of the titty binness."

And right then I realized what happened. I had Bubba Barclay get me out of jail on the Lake Quapaw deal by givin over all my remaining worldly belongings to Rhett Beavers, on account of they said he could sue me from here to Nome, Alaska, for screwin up his World Book binness, and with a little bit left over for Bobo Rodriguez, except they weren't ever able to find Bobo and so Rhett came on down, figured everthing out, and kept the binness going in my absence. None of this mattered, though, once I figured out that it really was him and that *this* was the man who aardvarked with my wife.

So I lit into Rhett like a pickax crackin open an Aunt Jemima pancake, grabbed onto his Frankie Avalon hairdo and ripped out a handful the size of Cleveland and then bulldogged him to the ground so hard he cost me 400 bucks in Aztec god candelabras. And all this time that I was grindin his skin into decorator wallpaper, all Rhett could do was yell "I never *touched* her, Joe Bob, it was *business*! I never *touched* her." And I heard him the first time, but I was having too much fun, and, besides, all the Meskin guys started throwing pesos down on the floor like at the cockfights and I was building up some pretty strong odds in the event that Rhett threw me out the window or something. Finally, though, I couldn't figure out a way to get a bet down, so I kicked his elbow and let him go.

You know, it's just amazing what kickin the crap out of somebody can do for your mood. I felt so much better that I stuck out my hand, helped him up, and said to him, "Still friends?"

I don't really know why. All I know is, once I found out he was only interested in José's tits for commercial reasons, I just couldn't hate him anymore. It was like learning your best friend has the same kind of coin collection you do. He was like a brother to me.

And then it hit me. *If Rhett was alive, then maybe, just maybe . . .*

"Is she . . . ?"

But Rhett already read my thoughts. He turned to me, shook his head quickly, looked away.

"They never found her," he said.

"Did they check all the spars?"

"Of course we checked spars," Rhett flared. "All the spar-clingers were rescued."

"And the funeral?"

"They never found the body, so we just had a little Lake Quapaw fish-fry service. Just me and a few of the World Book people. We would of called you, Joe Bob, but you were in jail."

"No body?" I was dying all over again.

"I know what you're thinking, Joe Bob, and, yes, it's possible."

"What's possible?"

"It's possible that her body suffered a direct hit from a bazooka-launched rocket, disintegrated into twelve thousand pieces, each one the size of a dime, and evaporated into the stratosphere."

"How'd you know that's what I was thinking?"

"It's kinda like Beanee Weenies."

"I guess *life* is kinda like Beanee Weenies."

And then we collapsed on each other and cried our little faces off, but then some of the customers started to leave and so we got control of ourselves and got back to business.

Rhett had everthing all figured out during the three days I was downriver. All of a sudden we couldn't get *enough* dozing-Meskin bookends. My whole supply was sold out the first day after I made Federico a free man, and for a while we thought the president of Mexico was gonna have to call out the Gorilla Guard to stop the rioting outside the El Mercado. Even after Rhett got in town and took charge, they damn near ripped down the pre-fab Dacron walls trying to get at those souvenirs, but Rhett, being a hell of a binnessman his ownself, convinced em that you didn't *necessarily* need a dozing-Meskin bookend to get to America. It was the *best* thing you could have—Federico proved that—but you could get by just using a rooster pinata and a Nehru. Then, if you wanted to be double sure they'd wave you through, you could buy a bullfighter's cape and/or the above-mentioned miniature snow scene, featuring two Meskins perched on a seesaw that said "I Love Acapulco." Where Rhett got those I have no idea, since I believe you normally have to buy em in Guadalajara.

Anyhow, we had us a binness partnership made in heaven. As soon as I sued Rhett to get my company back, we made a trip together down into the Yucatan Peninsula and hired some Indians to make dozing-Meskin bookends, ten for a peso, and then we turned around and *sold* those same bookends for 12 pesos apiece—18 if you got the one that had the "U.S. Immigration" sticker on the bottom of it. You figure it out. That's anywhere from 12,000 per cent profit to 18,000 per cent profit, depending on how we were doing in any given week.

We had people pouring into the shop from all over north Mexico, asking to see the *"el Mexicano snoro de biblio."* Some of em didn't even *want* to go to America till they found out how easy it was. And, by the hundreds, they were *proving* how easy it was. Sometimes you could go by the International Bridge late at night and there'd be thirty, forty Meskin families waiting to cross, all of em holding identical Dozing Meskin Bookends, "Kiss Me, I'm Stupid" T-shirts on the kids, and gold-sequin sombreros. Soon as they even got *close* to the border guards, sure enough they'd just wave em on through like cattle. Sometimes Rhett and me would have our chauffeur take us over to the bridge, just to watch our binness percolatin along, and we'd look at each other and smile and say, "This could go on forever."

Course, we had occasional problems. We had to buy out "Chess Sets Unlimited," cause the guy was starting to sell quartz chess sets for *eight pesos* and telling people chess sets would work just as good as Dozing Meskin Bookends. Not many people believed him, but one weekend the mayor's daughter, *la sluta de alcalde*, purchased a chess set and passed into Brownsville unmolested—the first day in four years she had gone unmolested—and so we lost a lot of binness the next few days and had to finally buy the sucker out just to avoid confusion.

But, you know, it seems it always happens this way, that you come up with a great idea, you establish a legitimate binness, and what happens? Somebody with less ethics than you tries to *take advantage*. People that don't have any integrity start *using* you like an old piece of sanitary napkin.

This is exactly what happened to me.

I don't remember when I first noticed it. Maybe it was Rhett that caught on first. I think somebody came into the store, said they wanted to buy just *one* dozing-Meskin bookend, when everbody knew damn well what our policy was, you gotta buy a *complete* set, two bookends per customer, no partial orders, in *spite* of the fact that Federico crossed the border with a single. (I can't tell you how many times I regretted not giving Federico a bookend in each hand. For years everbody said, "But what about Federico? How many bookends did Federico carry with him on San José Roberto Day?" And I'd have to say, "I *am* San José Roberto, you little slimeball," and then they'd kiss the hem of my garments and everthing would be okay.) Anyhow, some guy came in the store, wanted to buy one bookend, and when we told him the policy, he said, "But I already *have* the other one."

Rhett got kinda peeved, thought maybe we had another cheap-imitation competitor trying to rip us off, and was on the verge of calling up Consuelo Martini and telling him to send the Free Enterprise Tactical Squad to check out El Mercado and find out who was making the fake dozing-Meskin bookends. But then Rhett noticed that the bookend in question had the unmistakable hand-carved plastic seal of the Cancun Indians, which was the tribe that we had the peso-per-ten deal with, and so then he got really angry cause he was thinking employee theft, bootlegging, black market, all *kinds* of horrible possibilities.

"Just *where* did you get this Dozing Meskin Bookend?" Rhett demanded.

And the customer looked up at him and said, "From my cousin Enrico."

And Rhett said, "Enrico who and where can I find him?"

And the customer said, "Enrico Petkievich in East Moline, Illinois."

It took us a couple of hours to grill this guy and get to the bottom of it, but what we found out was this: Certain unscrupulous illegal aliens were purchasing dozing-Meskin bookends, using them to get to America, then *mailing them back to their relatives in Mexico for reuse.* In other words, they were paying *one time* for *multiple uses* of the same dozing-Meskin bookend, or burro paperweight, or what have you. They were dealing, in other words, in international souvenir piracy.

We were none too pleased to find this out. We went straight to Consuelo Martini and asked him what could be done, but he said it was out of his hands. When you got into international mail, you had to deal with *Federales.* Then, a couple weeks after the single-bookend customer showed up at the store, I noticed a slight drop-off in binness. Maybe it was just me, but at the peak we were selling maybe, oh, 38,000 dozing-Meskin bookends a week, and now I noticed it was down to 37,250.

I don't know what you would of done, but I wasn't about to sit around and let a bunch of ungrateful wetbacks ruin the life of my grandchildren. So I went over to Brownsville and hired me a lawyer and filed a federal lawsuit immediately and *reported* some of these people to the Border Patrol. What they were doing was "Illegal Repatriation of Burros, Sombreros, Meskin Snow Scenes, et al." We went and filed our complaint at all the agencies on the U.S. side *and* in Consuelo Martini's office, and I pretty much expected that to take care of it and was hoping the Meskin government would start inspecting that mail a little more carefully and start catching some of these souvenir pirates and putting em in the *carcel*.

But I think it says something about this country of ours that the federal government—*our* federal government, yours and mine—didn't do diddly to help an American binnessman in his time of need. You know what they did *instead*? They started questioning ever single person that walked across that bridge with a dozing-Meskin bookend in their hands. I tried to tell em they misunderstood. It wasn't *those* people that were cheating. It was the Meskins up in *Chicago* that were screwing everything up. But it seemed like the more I protested, the more they got it wrong. And finally, one day, Rhett came and got me and told me he had to close up the store—the Border Patrol turned *everbody* back that day and they were all demanding their money back and he would recommend we get out of town.

I probly would of took him up on it, too, but right at that moment some of Consuelo Martini's men came to the door and said, "Are you Mr. Briggs?"

And I said, "That's San José Roberto to you."

And they said, "I'm afraid we're going to have to extradite you to Corpus Christi."

And I said, "*¿Qué?*"

And they said, "The American government is demanding your extradition."

And I said, "On *qué* charge?"

And they said, "Conspiracy to smuggle aliens."

And I said, "I didn't conspire."

And they said, "Also importation of toxic souvenirs."

And I said, "What?"

And they said, "Some of those bookends had un-declared tamale shavings inside of them."

And I said, "You gonna hold me responsible for what rubbed off a bunch of stupid Cancun Indians while they were hand-molding the plastic?"

And they said, "Please come with us."

And I guess it was right after that they dumped me at the border and arrested me and threw me in the Corpus Christi jail.

Which just goes to show:

You spend all your life trying to make an honest buck, and then you lose everthing because of what some ignorant unsaved savage was eating one day.

15

How I Solved the Kennedy Assassination

It was while I was in the Corpus Christi Jail that I solved the Kennedy Assassination. I know it's a familiar story, so I'll just go over the outlines here. A lot of people don't realize that solving the Kennedy Assassination wasn't my first choice when I got to prison. For the first six months I was there, I pressed license plates by hand. Then I got a year added on to my sentence cause it's illegal to make license plates at that prison. While I was workin off my solitary, I learned to play blues guitar, harmonica, and tuba. Sometimes I would play blues tuba, but I had to stop cause all the black inmates were getting p.o.ed at me. After that I started collecting Fudgsicle sticks and building an Egyptian pyramid, but the warden put a stop to that. He said, in the future, if I wanted to build Egyptian pyramids in my cell, I would have to take the Fudgsicles off the sticks first. You can see the kind of constant persecution I had here, just like Burt Lancaster in *The Birdman of Alcatraz,* where he spends his whole life fighting the tweeter-haters.

I guess I'll always remember where I was when they told me President Kennedy was dead. I was in the Corpus Christi Jail and it was August 17, 1969. I guess I'd been doing about nine months worth of "time" (that's what we called it on the inside) before it hit me one day and I said, "Hey, I'm in prison. This is kind of interesting."

And my hard-boiled cellmate, a guy named "The Rock" cause his head looked exactly like a piece of crumbly shale with graffiti all over it, said, kinda sarcastic, "Yeah, they killed Kennedy, too."

"They did?"

Six years since it happened and *nobody told me.*

"What'll happen to Jackie?" I said.

And The Rock said something totally disgusting about Jackie's pillbox hat, and I had to attack his brass knuckles with my face in order to teach him a lesson.

It was while I was in the prison infirmary that I first started piecing the facts together. Here's what I was able to find out from newspaper accounts, library books, the complete report of the Warren Commission, and stuff I heard in the men's bathroom:

1. Kennedy and Jackie go to Dallas.

2. Kennedy gets sick on the plane, but nobody thinks much about it.

3. On final approach, Kennedy turns to Jackie and says, "Do you realize there are seven letters in 'Kennedy' *and* seven letters in 'Lincoln,' that Lincoln was killed on a Friday by a lone gunman shooting at the back of his head, and that Lincoln was succeeded by a Vice President named 'Johnson'?"

4. Jackie replies, "Oh, honey, don't be silly. A lot of names have seven letters. Like, oh, 'Onassis.' "

5. At 9:45 A.M., Lee Harvey Oswald reports to his job at the Texas School Book Depository and starts mouthing off about the "Fair Play for Aruba Committee," an extremist political group dedicated to the violent overthrow of tourist casinos in Venezuela. His co-workers ignore him. One of them says, "Fuck Aruba." No one notices that Oswald is

carrying a 32-millimeter semi-automatic Czechoslova-kian-made shoulder cannon.

6. At 11:47 A.M., JFK says, "Hey, let's take the convert-ible, what do you think?"

7. At 12:07 P.M., Secret Service Agent-in-Charge Ivan Vladimirovich Kunyetsov leans over to JFK and says, "Mr. President, John Connally says *he* wants to ride in the front seat." The President gets a pained expression on his face, but finally says, "Okay, but I get the front seat on the way back." (This part always brings a tear to my eye, because, of course, as we all know, there would be no "way back" that fateful day.)

8. At 12:14 P.M., the President tells his driver to stop so he can get out of the car, walk over to a young boy holding a "We Love You, Jack" sign, and give him a quarter. The boy stares up into the President's eyes, takes the quarter, and gives the President a plastic bag containing one-fourth ounce of marijuana.

9. At 12:19, as the motorcade rolls past the gaily deco-rated buildings on Main Street, Lee Harvey Oswald shoves nine crates of *Dick and Jane* readers and two crates of *This Wonderful World!* seventh-grade science books into position next to an unopened bag of French fries, left on the windowsill that will serve as his grisly lunch table. A co-worker happens by, notices Oswald erecting a telescopic sight for a laser-guided hand-held missile, and says, "Are you gonna eat those greasy fries? Yecccch!" Little did he know that Oswald would have no time for more than six or seven fries on this day.

10. As the President's limo approaches Dealey Plaza from the east, a right-wing photographer for the *Dallas Morning News* takes up his position atop the Triple Un-derpass, where he opens a camera case and starts care-fully unloading his venom.

11. At 12:31, the motorcade makes a complicated zig-

zag motion through Dealey Plaza, and at that moment
Jackie looks up at the Texas School Book Depository and
says, "Oh, look, isn't that a pretty Czechoslovakian shoulder cannon?" In the front seat, Governor John Connally
turns to his left so that he can speak over his shoulder to
the President and says, "You *always* get to ride in the
front."

12. At 12:32, Secret Service Agent Yuri Jakov jumps
onto the running board of the President's limousine,
jumps off again, and says, "Gee, this is fun."

13. At 12:33, an overweight man carrying an umbrella
stands at the corner of Elm and Houston, absent-
mindedly massaging the crotch of his trousers. Several
people notice, but say nothing.

14. At 12:34, in suburban Irving, Marina Oswald flips
through a yellowed copy of *Life* magazine, comes across a
photograph of Connie Francis, and feels a sudden sensa-
tion of horror and dread.

15. At 12:35, a manhole cover in the middle of Elm
Street, just 20 yards from the Grassy Knoll, goes unno-
ticed by everyone.

16. At 12:36, Abraham Zapruder presses the button on
his Bell & Howell home-movie camera and says, "I hope
Jackie has one of them strapless numbers on."

17. At 12:37, with the presidential limousine moving
forward at 11.2 miles an hour and approaching the Triple
Underpass, Lyndon Baines Johnson, two cars behind the
President, notices the unmistakable sound of a Czechoslo-
vakian shoulder cannon being fired rapidly. He says,
"They must be some good squirrel-huntin around here."

18. At 12:38, it's all over. The Prez disappears off the
map of human history.

19. At 12:41, Lee Harvey Oswald walks downstairs,
gathers together eight or nine of his co-workers, and says,
"I was just up there shootin off my shoulder cannon and I

accidentally killed the President." No one thinks this is odd.

20. At 12:49, Oswald decides to ride the bus to the Texas Theater and take in an Abbott and Costello double feature. He takes his pistol with him, in case they show the one where they land on Venus and start playing footsie with Anita Ekberg.

21. At 1:01 P.M., emergency-room doctors at Parkland Hospital diagnose the President as suffering from three gigantic shoulder-cannon wounds to the head and neck.

22. At 1:20, the opening titles roll for *Abbott and Costello Meet the Mummy.* Enraged, Oswald starts firing his pistol at the screen, killing a Dallas police officer in the process.

23. At 2:05, Jack Ruby, a Dallas nightclub owner, walks into the entertainment department of the *Dallas Times Herald* and says, "Wait till you see the titties on this one."

24. Two days later, Jack Ruby says, "Don't scrunch up the side of your face like that if you know what's good for you," and pumps three bullets into the abdomen of Lee Harvey Oswald. Oswald says, "I did it for Aruba." Nobody thinks this is odd.

25. Two weeks later, three casinos in Aruba close forever.

26. Four years later, the Warren Commission enters its final report. "One man, acting alone." Who that man was, we'll probly never know.

And that's basically the story we all know, the one we grew up with, the one they teach in school.

But is it the *whole* story?

No way, José.

No way, José Napoleon Duarte.

As I say, I had six months solitary to consider the facts of this case, then another two, three months in the infirmary, so I think I can say with authority that I'm the world's leading prison authority on the Kennedy Assassination, except for the people directly involved in the conspiracy, of course.

And I won't go into all my sources, except to say I read the following books in their entirety:

The President Is Dead! The President Is Dead! by Kurt Withers, former special assistant to the assistant district attorney, Dallas County, Texas.

The Assassination Please Almanac, edited by Tom Miller, the master himself.

Jack You Devil: My Life With Jack Ruby by Heather "Hooters" Lee.

How the Dirty Commies Did It by John Wayne, as told to Irving Reinfeld.

Conspiracy? Murder? Just a Guy With a Cannon? and Other Misleading Information About November 21, 1963 by Bob Woodward, as told to his wife, Babs.

Please Forgive My Bullet: What Really Happened Out There by Marina Oswald, as told to Mikhail Stepanovich Grigorin.

El Presidente Morte, de Manuel Olivares, Washington bureau chief for the respected *Diario Castro de Havana.*

Rush to Judgment by Mark Lane.

Highlights from Rush to Judgment by Mark Lane.

Another Rush to Judgment Book He Put Out Right After That One by Mark Lane.

The Warren Commission Report: Boy, Did Those Guys Blow It! by Stan Silver, Earl Warren's brother-in-law from Milwaukee.

Who Is Dealey Anyway? The Story of Dealey Plaza by Joe B. Dealey.

Who Screwed Up? by Jack "Dogface" Strindberg, special agent-in-charge, Dallas FBI assigned to the "Oswald, Lee Harvey" section.

He's Not Really Dead by Sister Mary Ignatius Candelaria, deceased.

It Sounded Like Squirrel Huntin to Me by Lyndon Baines Johnson.

And, of course, I went back and read all the back issues of *What Will They Dig Up Next?* the official journal of the assassination conspiracy binness, and based on all my research, I decided we had *quite a few* unanswered questions out there. Like:

Numero Uno: Who was really the President in 1963? They say Kennedy now, but it's been a long time and who can remember dates like that? Try this trick on yourself. Was Warren G. Harding President in 1914 or 1924? See? You don't know, do you? And it could mean a difference of *ten years* in our understanding of history. So take Kennedy, he could of been President in '53, '63, '73. Who the heck remembers now?

Numero Two-o: It's well known that many people keep Czechoslovakian-made shoulder cannons in the back of their pickups for routine weasel hunting. Why did Lee Harvey Oswald buy his in Russia?

Numero Three-o: Did Jackie really expect to get away with those shoes?

Course, I had to wait until my parole to actually go check out the Conspiracy situation up in Dallas, but once I did I made a beeline for the Oswald rooming house on Beckley Avenue, which is where I started my investigation. When I got there—and we're talking May 21, 1970, for all the historians in the audience—there were quite a few hippies living upstairs, throwing fairy dust on each other and watching Peter Fonda movies. As far as I know, these hippies have never been explained. But I questioned several of them extensively, researched all their astrological signs, and discovered that, of the 14 hippies living upstairs in the Oswald rooming house, 13 had never

heard of Lee Harvey Oswald. The 14th, a pale and sickly
woman named Lucille "Aqualung" Pisces, told me that on
the afternoon of November 22, 1963, she was attending
fourth-period classes at Vince Lombardi Junior High
School in Mason, Georgia. I subsequently traveled to the
aforementioned junior high and verified that the woman's
story was, in fact, correct. Lucille Pisces also entrusted me
with the information that one night, while rooting around
on the floor listening to Grateful Dead music and doing
"The Gator," she noticed one of those trick fountain pens
that have nekkid ladies inside the glass part, resting
against a windowsill, coated with cobwebs. On one side of
the pen, stamped in gold, it read:

Manny's Weapon Photography
We Make Your Gun Look Like a Member of "The Family"
403 W. Jefferson
"Don't Shoot, Just Toot"

At first glance it looked like just a plain old ordinary ad for
a gun-photo studio. They're all over that part of Dallas.
But then I remembered: Lee Harvey liked to have his
picture made with *all* his guns. It was kind of a hobby with
him. If this place was still there, then maybe, just
maybe . . .

"Sure I remember him," said Floyce Viridiana, a robust
woman who looked like she just loaned out her lower
body for trampoline practice. "He was the skinny kid that
always came in here mumbling about howitzer ammuni-
tion."

"What caliber?"

"Forty-sevens. What else?"

"That's him. And what did he want from you?"

"Just the usual. Pictures of him with his Mannlicher

pump-action with telescopic. Him with his .38 Smith & Wesson. Him with his Czechoslovakian shoulder cannon."

"Did you say Czechoslovakian shoulder cannon?"

"Right. You know, the kind they use for weasels."

"What did it have on it?"

"If I remember right, he had a laser-guided telescopic sight with a little engraving on top of it."

"An engraving?"

"Yeah. Something like 'This one's for you, Jack.' "

" 'This one's for you, Jack'?"

"Yeah. 'This one's for you, Jack.' We never could figure out what it meant."

"Probly something personal."

"I wouldn't know about that, Mr. Briggs."

So there I had my first clue. Evidently Oswald had traveled to the gun-photo shop on Jefferson Street with the *express* intention of having himself photographed with a Czechoslovakian shoulder cannon. We didn't know it was the *same* cannon yet. But we knew it had a distinctive marking on the telescopic sight. Now all we had to do was find this *Jack* guy.

"Thank you very much, Floyce. By the way, did you happen to keep the negatives of this picture of the Czech shoulder cannon?"

"Yes, sir, I always do."

"Would you mind if I took a look at those?"

"I'm sorry, sir, but that would be an ethics violation for those of us in the gun-pitcher binness. You know, sometimes people like to get *comfortable* with their gun, if you know what I mean, before we snap the picture."

"I suppose you're speaking of *in flagrante torpedo*?"

"That's right. I wouldn't wanta be responsible for somebody getting caught with their pump-loader exposed."

"No, ma'am, we wouldn't want that."

"Sorry."

"I don't guess you'd show it to me if I exposed my pump-loader, would you?"

After I had all the buckshot surgically removed from my hiney, I went on to the next phase of the investigation, which was to trace the origins of the slogan " 'This one's for you, Jack.' "

To do this I went directly to the Dallas Public Library and read the complete works of A.C. Greene, because A.C. Greene wrote all the books in the Dallas Public Library, beginning with *Famous Drunk Indians That Visited Dallas in the 1860's and Got Killed With Muskets*, continuing right on through *Dallas in the Eighties: Gimme Some Money*. What I was searching for was any book with a reference to this mysterious "Jack." I suppose I read books for durn near two weeks before I finally came to one solitary entry:

Jack Brangus, also known as "Jack" and "Hatrack Jack," Women's Clothing Department, Neiman-Marcus; accused in 1964 of physically attacking a boutique customer with a Masonite hatrack; cleared by the Dallas County Grand Jury after seven weeks of testimony; previously known as the designer of a white-satin rose-petal headdress once worn by Mae West; originated the slogan "Don't crochet with lamé."

That was it—*all* that was known about the man. But somehow, I don't know, I just had a hunch about Hatrack Jack, and so I set out to find him. I tried Neiman-Marcus, but nobody wanted to talk.

"Listen, buddy," said Sylvia Swanson, head of costume jewelry, "you ask too many questions about Hatrack Jack and you're gonna wish you hadn't."

"Oh yeah?" I said.

"Listen, I don't know if you've ever heard of black egret feathers fitted on a black velvet gown that flares at the knees and squeezes the bodice, but I saw that done to somebody one time and it's not a pretty sight."

"I think I heard about that case."

"Sure you did. Everybody did. Those egret feathers were famous. They knew a dress designer did it, or at least somebody *posing* as a dress designer. And I would say about 99 point 9 per cent of us thought it was Hatrack Jack."

"Is that right?"

"Not that we could ever prove anything, mind you."

"Sure."

"So you see what you're dealing with here?"

"Satin Lastex on an Esther Williams bathing suit?"

"Right. That kind of thing. Killer fabrics."

"I'll remember that."

But not all the Neiman's employees were so cautious. Finally, an assistant cashier in the Ridiculous Belts Department pulled me aside and said, "Hey, did I hear you asking about Hatrack Jack?"

"Maybe. What's it to you?"

"I know where you can find him."

"And it's gonna cost me, right?"

"That depends on you."

"Oh, yeah. Depends on me what?"

"Depends on whether you'll expose your pump-loader or not."

Three days later, I had the address I needed. It was a run-down tenement in East Dallas with a sign out front that said "Rooms for Free." As soon as I stepped inside, I felt like I was stepping into a run-down tenement in East Dallas.

"Anybody home?" I said.

Three rats convened a rodent convention under the stairwell and elected me the social director.

"Yoohoo! Anybody here?"

Upstairs I heard the unmistakable sound of pro basketball, as though ten massive bodies were jostling for a rebound. I made a few tentative steps up the stairs, then stopped with a jolt.

Suddenly the door at the top of the stairs swung open and a high-pitched, nasal voice said, "Somebody down there?"

"Yes, I'm looking for Mr. Hatrack Jack Brangus. Does he live here?"

There was a moment of silence, and then, "Wait just a minute."

I waited maybe ten minutes, and finally Mr. Brangus emerged from his room. He looked like he'd been making French toast.

"Sorry it took so long," he said. "I had a professional basketball team in my room."

"So I noticed."

"Soooooooooooooo. What can I do for you?"

I immediately noticed that Mr. Hatrack Jack Brangus put twelve extra o's in the word "so."

I said, "Depends on you."

"Well, I'm not exposing my pump-loader, if *that's* what you're after."

"No, no, nothing like that. All I need is a little information."

"Yeah."

"On Lee Harvey."

Suddenly Hatrack Jack's face turned the color of a three-day-old Hostess Twinkie.

"Not . . . not . . ."

"That's right, Brangus—Lee Harvey Oswald!"

Suddenly Hatrack Jack's arms turned the color of an engorged walrus.

"How did you find me?"

His voice sounded pathetic, like the sound of a baby hamster being forced into a Vienna Sausage can.

"So you know something, do you?" I said.

"Did they already tell you about the ostrich neck-ruffs and draped oversleeves?"

"Ostrich? I heard about some *egret* feathers."

"Not the ones on the lace Medici collars and seed-pearl arabesques!"

The man was crumbling into a little pile of catalogue copy, right before my very eyes, so I grabbed him by the collar and shook him and said, "Okay, Hatrack, get ahold of yourself. Whatever you got to say, you can say it to me. But I'm not leaving till I find out what's going on here."

He looked frightened by my manly brusqueness.

"Okay," I said, "let's start with these ostrich neck-ruffs."

He swallowed the lump in his throat, stared up at me with trembling eyes, and spilled his guts.

Before he started to confess, I made him go get a mop and pail and clean up his guts.

"The neck-ruffs were nothing really," he said. "It started innocently enough. One day I was hanging around Women's Jewelry and I picked up this set of pigeon-egg pearls. They were darling—you should of seen them. It was *nothing*. I mean who cares, right?"

"And what did you do with aforesaid pigeon-egg pearls?"

"I'm getting to that. I'm *getting* to it. Don't you see how hard this is for me? Don't you have just a *little* compassion for a man in my position?"

"Okay, okay."

"So what happens? The woman behind the counter, a dear dear woman, Aubrey Bohannon Davies, she says to me, 'Have you seen the white lacquered wig we have to go with those?' You know, just kidding around. She didn't mean anything by it. And then . . . and then . . . I don't know if I can do this."

"Brangus, you're gonna tell me what you did with those pigeon-egg pearls and that white lacquered wig or else we're gonna march over to Stanley Marcus's house and you're gonna have to tell *him.*"

"No, no, not that. Okay, okay, I'll talk. . . So I put on the pearls."

"You *what*?"

"It was just *one* little string of pigeon eggs. At least at first."

"And what about later?"

"Do we have to go into all of it?" he whined.

"All of it."

"Then I put on the white lacquered wig and did the Dance of the Seven Veils."

"Right there in the store?"

"Right there in the store. You know, just horsing around."

"Without any *music*?"

"Right. No music. No warning. I just put on the wig and started doing the Dance of the Seven Veils."

"You expect me to believe that?"

"I don't care if you believe it or not. It happens to be true."

"What did you use for veils?"

"Peacock feathers."

"Not *real* peacock feathers."

"No no, of course not. That was much later. Imitation peacock feathers."

"And what happened when you did the Dance of the Seven Veils?"

"Nothing at first. That's why it was so *seductive*. Nobody seemed to mind. Aubrey didn't mind. Phil *certainly* didn't mind."

"Who's Phil?"

"He used to get the peacock feathers for me."

"Oh."

"But then it started to become a sickness. I don't know how it happens. One day it's pigeon-egg pearls and pea-cock feathers, the next day it's embroidered chiffon and ruby-stone berry beads. You don't know what's happening to you. I used to excuse myself three or four times a day, go into the private dressing rooms, and get a taffeta fix. I remember one time I was so deep into 'dressing-up' that I wrapped a red velvet evening gown, with white ermine collar and cuffs, in a gold-foil package so we could go in the back and 'play Santa Claus.' "

"That's *disgusting.*"

"But you must understand. It's a disease. It's beyond your control. You get to a point where you have to sniff the chinchilla twice a day or else you get the shakes. Have you ever seen a silk-brocade junkie with Joan Crawford shoulders?"

"No, can't say that I have."

"The shoulders get that way from constant exposure to laurel-leaf epaulets. Some people get permanent spinal injuries. I've seen two cases of paraplegia."

"And this really happened to you? You were that far gone?"

"Are you kidding? I used to go over to Cosmetics and *beg* for porcelain makeup on my eyelids. That was after I got into the heavy stuff—Harlow white-satin halter necks, marabou stoles, bugle-bead skullcaps. And, of course, so much chiffon I can't even remember. Chiffon is the worst. There's no way to stop once you get started. You either run out of money or you run out of chiffon. That's the only way you'll get off the stuff."

"So you were drowning in chiffon?"

"Honey, I was *swathed* in it."

"So how did it all end?"

"It ended"—and he looked at me with fear and dread, like I was a used wool pants suit on the discount rack at K mart—"with the Assassination."

Could I have a little hokey Jack Webb music here please?

"Just as I thought," I said.

"I had this customer. 'Dorothy Lamour.' That wasn't her real name, of course, it's just what we called her. She'd come in two, three times a week, usually wrapped in sarongs. A beautiful woman. A real dear. Ostrich fronds out the kazoo. Anyway, Dorothy would come in and model spangled organdy for the children on Saturdays. That's the kind of person she was. But she was a strange person in other ways. She had a temper. She could get bent out of shape over little things, like whether it's okay to put pleated ruffles on butterfly sleeves."

"I wouldn't exactly call that a *little* thing."

"Well, no, that's not a very good example. But one time she was looking at a leopard-print crepe and considering it for the accessories that go with a black-satin ensemble, and I said, 'Honey, we're talking beauty disaster,' and she flew into an absolute rage over it. But I ask you, was I wrong? Leopard-print crepe with black satin. Of course I was right."

"It does sound like she was a little cockeyed."

"Okay, so you see what I was dealing with. But there was one subject we could never, never, *ever* mention around Dorothy."

"Yeah?"

"And that was Jacqueline Kennedy."

"Jackie?"

"Dorothy thought she was a fashion reptile."

"You're speaking figuratively, of course?"

"No, Dorothy was of the opinion that Jackie hunted flies with her tongue when it came to dressing for dinner."

"I see."

"It first started with the whole Oleg Cassini thing. Jackie would go to Paris and come back with these aquamarine frocky things, and Dorothy would be *hysterical* for a week. We'd have to use ermine to get her revived. Then, you probably remember what happened next."

"The pillbox hat?"

"Right. Dorothy started hyperventilating, and we had to tickle her soles with a feather boa. But even *that* wasn't the thing that did it. It was the shoes."

"I knew it."

"Jackie Shoes were too much for her. The first time I saw those pink pumps, I knew Dorothy would be coming in, ready to blow. But the strange thing about it, this time she just kind of sailed in and didn't say a word. She wandered over to Accessories, fingered a few alligator handbags, and then let out a big sigh. I knew what was on her mind, and so I said, 'Dorothy, I wouldn't get too upset. The woman is entitled to wear . . .' But Dorothy put her finger over my lips and said, 'Don't worry, dear, I've already handled it.' That was the last day I saw her."

"What? That's all?"

"The President came to Dallas three weeks later, and I guess you know the rest."

Hatrack started to sob. *"I could have stopped her. I could of done something."*

"Now, now, it's not your fault," I told him. "Besides, we don't *know* that it has any connection."

"Oh, she wanted to kill her all right. She *despised* those square bodices. She would of done anything to get rid of that woman."

"Are you saying the woman known as 'Dorothy Lamour' actually pulled the trigger?"

"Pulled it, hired somebody to pull it, paid Castro to pull it—what difference does it make? Our President is dead."

"Hatrack?"

"Yes."

"Do you know where Dorothy Lamour is today?"

"Runs a weapon-photo studio down on West Jefferson."

"*What?!*"

"Why, you know the place?"

"Does she look like she rents out the lower half of her body for trampoline practice?"

"Sure, that's the woman. Floyce something."

"Floyce Viridiana. She's *Aruban.* She has ready access to photographs of guns. And do you know what she carved on Lee Harvey Oswald's Czechoslovakian shoulder cannon?"

"What?"

" 'This one's for you, Jack.' "

"Oh my God!" cried Hatrack Jack, and apparently it was all the heart of this sad little man could handle. At that exact moment, he suffered a massive heart attack and collapsed into my arms. He would never live to dangle another bangle.

I don't know why I never turned Floyce in. By that time I guess I'd fallen in love with her. I drove back out to Jefferson Street, parked my car, tried to summon up the courage to go inside and tell her I knew about Hatrack Jack, but something about the guy's story had pierced through me. There was a sadness about it, something that said, "Okay, okay, the lady was right. Everybody *hated* those shoes." There was a certain justice to the whole deal, especially since the wishes of Floyce Viridiana had been frustrated by God. He took our President, but he freed Jackie to shop again. What the heck, I thought. It's no skin off my nose. And until now, I never told a soul what I found out in the little East Dallas tenement that day. But I would always remember the great lesson of the Kennedy Assassination:

Never mix textured fabrics with paisley.

16

How I Learned to Sin with Fat Girls, or Rock Bottom

This part's gonna be real hard for me.

After you solve the Kennedy Assassination, you spend a lot of time sittin around the house saying stuff like, "Why'd I do that?" In my case, I spent three years grieving for my vanished *el Presidente* and nursing the guilt over my failure to turn in Floyce Viridiana. For the first time in my life, I started drinking heavily. I'd drink anything—Scotch, bourbon, Mountain Dew. Sometimes I'd hang around the Dobbs House and wait for people to leave so I could go over and suck their ice. One night, after watching *Stranglers of Bombay* in Stranglescope at the Linda Kay Drive-In, I started drinking in a bar in Seagoville, drank my way up Highway 67 to a gas station in Cumby, sucked the Ethyl nozzle dry, and got arrested the next morning in Hooks, Texas, for drinking my way down a federal highway instead of using a car. You know, you stare at the bottom of a glass long enough and it changes you. It makes you cross-eyed, for one thing. You start doing things you wouldn't ordinarily do—like moving to Lawton, Oklahoma.

That's what happened to me. I admit it. I lived in Lawton, Oklahoma, for *three years.* Nobody knew that until now. Those are the years you've heard about all your life. The "dark years." The "forgotten years." The "whatever the heck happened to Joe Bob Briggs" years. That's right. I was in Lawton, hanging around Fort Sill, trying to join the Army. They wouldn't take me. They said it wasn't anything personal, it was my politics. I was a "conscientious sustainer." I went down to the draft board right at the heart of the Vietnam War and told em I didn't wanna go to Vietnam. They already had enough young American meat over there. I wanted to go to *France* and start blowing those people away for sending us Maurice Chevalier. I was one of the first conscientious sustainers to come out for total global warfare against everbody that couldn't prove he was American, specially the Frenchies. I told em, "Hey, what you're talkin in Southeast Asia is just quagmire. What you need is a *swamp.*" This was long before the Nixon deal, where we had *all kinds* of people trying to take credit for escalation. Anyhow, it wasn't a popular position at the time, so later, when I tried to join the Army due to my being a drunk, they said I was no longer eligible and then they assigned me to a counselor who suggested I should go to Canada.

It was just one more setback in this blackest period of my life. I guess it was shortly after that when I fell into a deep coma and started writing country-western songs. It was one of those "automatic writing" deals, like God started zapping me with these lyrics about my personal religious and spiritual self, and I had no choice but to send off to Nashville for the Chet Atkins Home-Study Guitar Course, and before you know it I was the opening act for The Prom Queens Plus One at the Holiday Inn lounge in Wichita Falls, Texas. Course, I didn't get there overnight. I struggled up through the ranks, working the honkytonks, the roadhouses, and worst of all, the sidewalk-houses. But I'll never forget the night when I was discovered by The Prom Queens Plus One. It was in Quanah, Texas, at a motel called Stop Here Rooms. I was working the late show for my "regulars," all the unemployed refinery workers from down in Electra. They'd drive up once a week just to watch me sing and shout out things at me, like, *"Yeeeeowwwww."* This was kind of a trademark with me. Everwhere I'd go, that's what people would yell. *"Yeeeeowwwww."* Always the same way, too, with four e's and five w's. It was the w's that made it different. Anyway, I was getting ready to do my pain-and-hurt song, the one I wrote in memory of José, when I noticed a mob forming at the back of the club. It was not a mob really. It was just the four fattest lounge singers in America. You know em already as Lucinda, Belinda, Donner, and Blitzen, the singing Maytag sisters, better known as The Prom Queens. (This was in the years before they hooked up with Hal "The Animal" Wilson and added authentic Hopi snake dances to their act.)

I tried to control my excitement. I fiddled with my guitar strings for a few seconds, causing the crowd to get restless and say, "Hey, I'm restless." I felt a lump in my throat, and for a moment I thought I had throat cancer. There was something growing in the pit of my stomach. It was a poorly digested burrito. I knew this was one of those magic moments in the history of show binness. It was like that night in '52 when the star broke her leg and Shirley MacLaine went on and did "Steam Heat" and started making a fool of herself professionally. It was like the first night Big Wayne Donka-Shaned publicly. I gave it the best intro I could think of:

"Here's a little song I wanna do for you now."

I knew that would grab em.

"I wrote it a few months back, for the woman that broke me in half. Her name was José. It's called 'When Orkin Comes to Spray.'"

There was an audible sound rustling throughout the

audience. I ignored it. And then, in the next four minutes, history was made. Here's the way it went.

When Orkin Comes to Spray
COPYRIGHT 1972, JOE BOB BRIGGS
I Wrote It, I Sang It, It's Mine, Don't Steal It

I been thinkin bout our trailer
And the way it used to sway
When the bedsprings started squealin high
And the roaches ran away . . .
But now you're gone to Memphis
In my brand-new Chevrolet—
Lord, I still feel you
When Orkin comes to spray.

When Orkin comes to spray, I roll the bed out
And underneath there I still see your eyes—
You left em there along with all your makeup,
Your Maybelline, your lipstick, and your lies.

(wail this part; make it hurt)
Your Maybelline, your lipstick, and your lies!
Mary Kay cannot apologize
For what you did to me in Waxahachie
The night Max Factor offered up your thighs.

(bring it back down; second verse)
I been thinkin bout our bathroom
And the way it used to smell
When you put on your cheap perfume,
Your Avon and Chanel . . .
But now it's full of sticky, plastic
Tubes of liquid Prell—

You even took the Lifebuoy!
Now you can go to hell!

(start crying here)
When Orkin comes to spray I roll the bed out
And underneath there I still see your eyes—
You left em there along with all your makeup,
Your Maybelline, your lipstick, and your lies.

(the talking verse)
I been thinkin bout our water bed
And the way it used to leak
When you put on your fingernails
And plunged em through our sheets . . .

But now you're popping beer tabs
With the nails that punctured me—
I hope he's got insurance
Or a Revlon factoreeeeeeeee.

(take it home)
When Orkin comes to spray I roll the bed out
And underneath there I still see your eyes—
You left em there along with all your makeup,
Your Maybelline, your lipstick, and your lies.

All I can say is, when I finished that song, there wasn't a
dry mouth in the house. I guess it took about a half hour to
restore order to the room and mop up the floors. And The
Prom Queens, they were knocked out by it. They wanted
to sign me up immediately, and they were so happy that
they didn't even want to press charges for being knocked
out.

That's how it happened. That's how I became the opening act for the heaviest act in show binness.

From that moment on I was constantly on the road. I watched *Gypsy* 12 times and called up my mama back in Frontage Road and begged her to come on the road with me and make like Rosalind Russell and strop me with a bullwhip until I became a star. She said uh-uh. I always thought she set me back five, six years when she said that. We worked Waukegan, we worked Syracuse, we worked Tuscaloosa. We even worked some places I knew how to pronounce. And everwhere we went, I did "Orkin" for the crowds. After a while, I even got billing on the poster-cards they tacked up out at the registration desk. I saved all of em. I keep em in my glove compartment:

TONIGHT ONLY!
THE PROM QUEENS PLUS ONE
Direct from Broken Arrow, Oklahoma
where they broke all house records and broke the house!
Singing! Dancing! They're fat!
Special Added Attraction: Stan Smith

That was me. "Stan Smith." I don't know why I chose that for my stage name. I guess I knew I was going some-where with a name like that. It was short, punchy, a name everbody always remembered. Sometimes I'd be leaving the club late at night, after the bar was closed, and there'd be people standing out by the stage door, just waiting there, wanting to talk to me. They'd say, "Hey, are you the guy that sings 'Orkin'?"
And I'd say, "Why, yes. Yes I am."
And they'd say, "That's what I *thought.*"
This would happen all the time. I can't tell you what it meant to me. And sometimes they'd bring their friends, so they could say, "I *told* you this is the guy. Lock at him. Don't he look like somebody that would sing about bug repellent?"

And I'd say, "The name's Smith. *Stan* Smith."

They loved me.

But, you know, in other ways it could be a lonely life, too. Strange towns, strange people, strange marks on the sheets. Ever night a new motel room, some nights a new motel. It could get pretty scary, just sitting around eating Colonel Sanders and watching the juice stain on the TV set get bigger while practicing my tuba. I used to work out all my new songs on the tuba before I'd sing em. Then I'd call all the Prom Queens to come into my room, then I'd ask em to get out of my room so I could breathe, and then we'd all go outdoors and I'd perform the new songs for em.

The Prom Queens really started to like me. They kept suggesting that we make a Dagwood sandwich together, with me as the baloney, but I'd just say, "No, sorry, I couldn't do anything like that. I might fracture my clavichord." And they always understood. Except for Blitzen. We had to tie her up at night so she wouldn't get loose, break down my door, and start whinnying passages from *The Black Stallion* to get my attention.

Looking back on it, it was something I needed at the time—four fat girls living next door. But there always seemed to be something missing. Sometimes it would get to me and I would realize that I had two choices: rip my face off with my fingernails, or write a song. So most of the time I'd write songs. I guess it was in the wintry winter of '73 that I wrote my first prison song. It was called "The Ballad of the Death Row Vegetarian," and it was reminiscent of those two long weeks I spent on Death Row in Arkansas before they took my Bass Monster. It went something like this:

(sing in low Johnny Cash voice)
Oh, the warden came a-callin on that lonely
   Wednesday night

And he asked me would I like a bite to eat
And I tole him, "I'll have Campbell's Soup and a little
*   diet Sprite,*
Cause I can't allow that poisonous red meat."

He said, "Joe Bob, I have brought you an enormous
*   rib-eye steak*
And I would suggest you eat it while you can"—
I said, "Warden, I can't do it, hear me out,
*   for goodness sake,*
I'm a health nut and a vegetarian."

(chorus)
At six A.M. *they're killin me, but I won't help em out,*
They can keep all their cholesterol at home,
Eight thousand volts ain't got a chance against a
*   brussel sprout,*
The chair can't kill a perfect chromosome.

Well, the warden, he kept pluggin, he said, "Joe Bob,
*   you are wrong*
If you think you're gonna make a fool of me—
I will starve you till you beg me to force-feed you with
*   Ding Dongs—*
Don't test me with your dang philosophy."

I said, "It's not just a theory that requires me to refuse
To consume your filthy cancer-causin grub—
And I intend to prove it when you throw the
*   final fuse,*
If I was you I'd hide behind a shrub."

At six A.M. *they're killin me, but I won't help em out,*
They can keep all their cholesterol at home,

*Eight thousand volts ain't got a chance against a
    brussel sprout,*
The chair can't kill a perfect chromosome.

*They led me out at five o'clock, put shackles on my
    feet,*
Then they shaved off all my healthy protein hair,
*But when they flashed some Fritos and said, "Joe Bob,
    you should eat,"*
I wheeled on them and shouted, "Don't you dare!"

*I said, "I have spent my lifetime taking care of my
    physique,*
And I'm not about to throw it all away—
If you really wanna help me, get a lentil and a leek
And drop them in a broccoli soufflé."

At six A.M. they're killin me, but I won't help em out,
They can keep all their cholesterol at home,
*Eight thousand volts ain't got a chance against a
    brussel sprout,*
The chair can't kill a perfect chromosome.

*The priest said, "Do you have now any final words
    to say?"*
The warden said, "Good riddance to this fool"—
But I said, "Yes, I would like one last vitamin called A
To ensure the health of all my molecules."

*The warden shouted, "Pull the switch!" and the lights
    they got real dim—*
But I swear to God, I didn't feel a thing—
It shorted out, exploded, and set fire to all of them,
For me it changed my voice so I could sing . . .

At six A.M. *they're killin me, but I won't help em out,*
They can keep all their cholesterol at home,
Eight thousand volts ain't got a chance against a
  brussel sprout,
The chair can't kill a perfect chromosome.

You would think with a song like that I'd have everthing in life I ever wanted, but you'd be surprised how unhappy I was musically. On the outside maybe I looked like a highly successful warm-up act for a herd of Brangus feed-lot cattle, but on the inside I was still a little pile of Cream of Wheat getting ice cold cause it slopped over on the grits. I would go through phases. Sometimes I wanted to chuck it all, go to Vegas, and be a pit boss. But then I'd give that up because I never could find out what a pit boss was. At other times I wanted to sail around the world in a bass boat. But most of the time, I guess, I just wanted to be a black person. I knew that if I could study hard and become a black person, then someday I'd be able to make a living by having the blues all the time. One weekend, when we were playing the La Petit Roche Club in downtown Little Rock, I took off a few hours and drove out Highway 10 to Panky, Arkansas, which is a resettlement camp for Negro tap-dancing families, but once I got there I was denied admission at the gate. And do you know what they said to me? I couldn't believe it. I was never so humiliated in my life. Do you know what they said to me?

They said, "Yo ain't black."

They didn't even make it rhyme.

After that I started singing the blues a lot and getting regular citations from the Association of Colored People Licensed to Sing the Blues, but by that time I didn't care. They knew they couldn't put me in prison cause I'd just write another prison song. So a lot of times, when I knew there weren't any Negro cops around, I'd just belt out a blues song and to hell with the consequences. I guess my best one was a cry-your-eyes-out standard called "The Dirt Mine Blues." It went like this:

(sing in loud Negro voice)
I got the dirt mine blues,
I'm blue as I can be. . . .
I got the dirt mine blues,
The grime done stuck to me. . . .
I got scuffed-up shoes
And skin like ebonyyyyyyy.

I got the low-down nasty filthy slimy scummy dirt
mine blues . . .
I got the low-down nasty filthy slimy scummy dirt
mine blues . . .
I got mud on my toenails and earthworms in my shoes.

Oh, I got the dirt mine blues,
They call me Cesspool Joe,
I got the dirt mine blues,
My sewers overflow,
I ain't Howard Hughes
No, all I am is Po.

I got the scumbag rotten awful Gross Out City dirt
mine blues . . .
I got the scumbag rotten awful Gross Out City dirt
mine blues . . .
I got a garbage-dump life that's settlin down in the
ooze.

I got the dirt mine blues,
My wife, she feed me swill,
I got the dirt mine blues,

I guess she always will,
That bitch puts slop on the table,
Just the smell of that stuff would make you ill.

I got the rootin tootin air-pollutin rat-recruitin dirt
    mine blues
I got the rootin tootin air-pollutin rat-recruitin dirt
    mine blues
I got rocks in my lunchbox and dirt-clod I.O.U.s.

(count it off)
Some days I'm a black man,
Some days I'm a brown,
Some days you can't make me out
Unless I'm upside down . . .
I got the dirt mine blues,
Blue as I can be . . .
I got the dirt mine blues,
The grime done stuck to me . . .
I ain't a nude mud wrassler,
Just a reasonable facsimileeeeeee.

(drive it home)
I'm dirty in the mornin,
Dirty at night
The only way to clean me
Is to lick me in a fight.
I got the dirt mine blues,
Blue as I can be . . .
I got the dirt mine blues,
The grime done stuck to me . . .
I got scuffed-up shoes
And skin like ebonyyyyyyyyyy.

I got so good at singing this song that sometimes all the white people in the room would start snapping their fingers like idiots, or try to rub their tummy and scratch their crotch at the same time. One time, when I was doing this song at the Club Riverbottom in Heloise, Tennessee, three people started crying, wailing, and caterwauling like serpents. Afterwards they came down to the front and told me they had just converted from Pentecostal to Negro. They asked me to pray with em and heal their skin, but I have to admit—and I'm not proud of this, even though I'm gonna tell you about it—I was such a pathetic piece of singing crapola that I just said, "Get away from me, you tongue-talkin bohunkies."

After that I started to get more and more bitter. I'd go for weeks without talking to The Prom Queens, or if I did talk to em, it would just be to say something like, "Hey, Fatso, can the Velveeta, how bout it?" I started studying the complete Mel Torme Songbook just so I could terrorize audiences *for the fun of it.* Once I didn't shave for eight weeks, and after that I just shaved one side of my face and dunked the other side in a vat of Aqua Velva.

No, don't feel sorry for me. I wanted to do it. I *loved* the pain.

I started keeping pornographic books in my room. I started out with *Jonathan Livingston Seagull* and worked up to the "hard stuff." By the end of '74 I was reading *Love Story* over and over again, learning the "good parts" by heart.

I was sinking fast. It was during this period of my life, the period I call "Stupid," that I wrote the song that ended it all for me. The song that was banned in thirty-seven states and one foreign country (Madagascar) and the Vatican. The song that was never heard by most of the known civilized world. I don't have any excuse for it, I guess. All I can say is I wrote it when I got to the point when it was obvious I was never gonna be any of the things I wanted to be in life. I wasn't getting any younger, after all, and I wasn't getting any older either, which confused me. I was banned from the titty-bar binness, due to a "no-compete" contract I had to sign with my close friend Rhett Beavers. I was banned from the immigration consultant binness, due to a "no-compete" contract I had to sign with Mad Dog Wallace of the U.S. Border Patrol. The world refused to hear my solution to the Kennedy Assassination. There was no José, of course. But worst of all, there were times when, late at night, I could hear The Prom Queens in the next room, *shaving their legs.*

I ask you. What would you do? All I did was write the song that has been kept from the ears of the world until now. Right now. You're about to hear it. Well, you're not really gonna hear it, but you're about to read it, and believe me, that's better than hearing it. It's called:

You Said You Were a Virgin, but Your Baby Ain't Named Jesus

(vamp)
In 1972 we found each other,
In 1973 we had a ball,
In 1974 we got a preacher,
But in 1975 I learned it all . . .

You said you were a virgin but your baby ain't named
    Jesus
Now you're gonna suffer all the consequence
Cause I thought you were mine alone, but you have
    twelve diseases—
You entrusted me with all the evidence.

*You got little boys in Nashville, little girls in Kansas
   City,*
They named a day-care center after you,
*But now it's time to lay it on the line and it's not
   pretty,*
It's time to send your hormones to the zoo.

(cry your eyes out)
You told me you were holy!
But not a holy cow,
I didn't know you worked at Owens Farms,
The preacher never tole me
That the good Lord would allow
The devil to possess such tender arms.

*They don't teach you in Sunday School what you
   taught me in bed,*
I shoulda known it when you greased me up,
*You lathered up my private parts with Kraft Cheese
   Topping Spread*
And then you left me nowhere to erupt.

*You said you were a virgin but your baby ain't named
   Jesus*
Now you're gonna suffer all the consequence,
*Cause I thought you were mine alone, but you had
   twelve diseases—*
You entrusted me with all the evidence.

I'm hiring me a lawyer!
He cost me ninety smackers
But it'll all be worth it in the end—
He tole me when a woman
Marries all the Green Bay Packers,
There is nothin in her virtue to defend.

You said you were a virgin but your baby ain't named
    Jesus,
You put the hurt on my intelligence,
Cause you said you were mine alone, but you had
    twelve diseases—
This wise man won't be bringin frankincense.

I first sang it on Christmas Day, 1975, at the Antioch Babtist Church of Willhoit, Missouri. Of course, I didn't realize it at the time, but I was possessed of Satan. I meant ever word of it.

I guess you could say I was a lost man. I couldn't even find The Prom Queens.

17

Salvation, Miracles, and the Meaning of Life

I don't guess I'll ever remember when it happened, where it happened, or why it happened. I just know it happened. There I was, sitting in the Holiday Inn lounge, Wichita Falls, Texas, at 6:27 P.M. on February 27, 1976, playing my guitar for a Weedeater salesman, and I was all set to do my closing number, which was always the same: "Chain Me Up and Beat Me, There Ain't Nothin Left to Love." So I started in on it, I wasn't more than eight or nine bars along, and this woman walks in that looks like she just got released from the Texas State Hospital for the Criminally Flat-chested, and I said to myself, "This lady could fry up sausage on her dental plates." That's how tough she looked. It shook me up so much that by the time I got to the final chorus, my voice was quavering and the cigarette was about to fall out of my mouth. What with all the reverb I had built into my Mister Microphone, it didn't sound too swift. But then I noticed somethin funny.

The lady was cryin her eyes out. She realized, at that very moment, that she was in the presence of a true artist. Either that or her panty hose were three sizes too little.

I was so touched that I decided to read from the World Book that night. Yes, I had kept the "R" volume. And at least once a day I read an entire article out of it to an unsuspecting audience, in memory of José. Today's selection was "Rickets."

Brushing a tear aside, I began: "Vitamin D plays an important role in the metabolism of calcium and phosphorus. In its absence, the deposition in the bones of the inorganic salt calcium phosphate (responsible for bone rigidity) does not proceed normally . . ."

But something strange was happening. Normally when I did my nightly World Book reading, everbody in the lounge would get up and leave. Tonight that wasn't happening. Tonight everyone was leaving except the lady at the table. She was listening with rapt attention.

"Cod liver oil and sunlight are helpful curing rickets in humans . . ."

I turned the sodden, yellowed page, still smelling of bass, but I couldn't continue. I closed the book, holding the place with my thumb.

"Excuse me," I said to the lady, "but haven't I slept with you before?"

She jumped a little bit and looked around like a deer on the first day of season.

"You must be mistaken," she said primly, and then she stared straight at me, like I was gonna know what to do next.

"Unless treatment is begun early," I said, suddenly finding it hard to concentrate, "rickets may produce such conditions as bowlegs, knock-knees, and a beady appearance of the ribs at their juncture to the breastbone."

I glanced up from the book, hoping she would still be there. The word "breastbone" echoed through my brain.

Slowly she begin to rise from her chair. She looked oddly familiar, but something was wrong.

"Maybe you'd like somethin besides 'rickets,' " I said to her. "How about 'Rochester'?"

She dropped her purse on the table and stepped to the side.

" 'Rhesus monkey'?" I stammered.

She cast her eyes down, as if wondering what to do now. I didn't know whether she would run away, bust out laughin, or just keel over like a mackerel. All I knew is I couldn't stand the humiliation of *her* leaving, too.

"How bout 'Paul Revere'?"

Suddenly, she reached for her blouse and yanked it up over her head, ripping her bra off as she did so. The sound I heard was unmistakable:

Thwack.

"José!" I screamed. *"José! José! José!"*

I jumped down off the stage and charged her like a bull elephant. I bear-hugged her to the fake linoleum and started rootin around like a trained attack pig. It was just like old times.

"But where?" I asked her between snorts. "Where have you been?"

"Searching for the 'R' volume," she gasped.

We both broke into tears. I grabbed her tits, groped at them wildly. It had been too long, far far too long.

"Joe Bob," she said at last.

"Yes?"

"I never blew up my tits for anybody else."

"No one?"

"No one."

"Not even Rhett?"

"Rhett was all business. We had a non-combustion contract. There were no fireworks at all. Until, of course . . ."

"Until what?"

"Until *you* brought them back to me. At Lake Quapaw. I'll never forget it. After the headfirst tackle, I was so scorched in the fire that I needed plastic surgery over ninety per cent of my body."

"That would explain it!" I shouted. "That would explain why you don't look like a bullfrog with acne anymore!"

"I'm a new woman."

"Tits are the same, though."

"Yes, the tits will always be the same."

"They're originals. The first. The most talented tits in the U.S.A. But, José, I've been searching for you, looking all over the world, spendin my life's savings. Where have you been?"

"Running. Running away and selling World Book while I did it."

"And are you still running?"

"Not any more. My legs are tired. I don't have the stamina."

"Thank God."

"I'm yours, Joe Bob."

"Mine."

"I'm Miss Largemouth Bass 1966, and I'm yours."

My heart did a Cherokee rain dance and ran for Congress in Utah. I hoisted José up by her armpits and noticed she had cellulite on her left thigh. I twirled her around like a flamingo caught in a commercial blender. I ripped her clothes off and sold out the late show.

After we posted bond on a charge of doing a live sex act at a late show at a Holiday Inn in Wichita Falls, Texas, which in Texas carries the possibility of death by lethal injection, we were able to settle down to a normal life in Bossier City, Louisiana. Just me, José, the fat girls, a couple pit bulldogs, an anaconda that people paid fifty cents to look at, and seventeen sets of World Books.

It was a simple life we had there. José's tits were tired and retired. I was no longer interested in becoming filthy rich, so I just laid around the house all day and let her cook for me like God intended. And sometimes I'd write a song or watch a game on the tube or send out for pizza or kick one of the fat girls across the room. It was, in many ways, a perfect life for me and José. And it was based on something a whole heck of a lot stronger than either one of us. It was the only household in America where Drive-In Jesus Is Lord.

That's why José kicked me out.

I'm gonna need a whole nother book to tell about it.

ABOUT THE AUTHOR

Joe Bob Briggs is a nationally syndicated movie critic whose column, "Joe Bob Goes to the Drive-In," is printed in some of the sickest newspapers in America. He is a regular host on The Movie Channel, occasionally hits the road with a show called "An Evening With Joe Bob Briggs," and on extra-special occasions, presents drive-in extravaganzas featuring himself, movie stars, himself, movies, himself, and his beloved Dancing Bovina Sisters. Billed as the world's largest chorus line, the Dancing Bovina Sisters are eight girls with a combined weight of 2200 pounds who can tap-dance, sing Joe Bob's original songs, and sit on one another in interesting shapes.

To get Joe Bob's "We Are the Weird" newsletter, which he bills as the only uncensored publication in America, write Joe Bob Briggs, P.O. Box 33, Dallas, TX 75221. If you send for it, enclose your answer to the following question: Should Joe Bob dump José and find some more tits to enslave him, or should he *grow up* and develop into a sensitive human being capable of adult relationships? If you want to be Joe Bob's next ex-wife, send a photo so he can do an ugly check.